How To Make It In The Music Business Using Social Media Marketing To Build A Large Following

Ousala Aleem

ISBN: 9781521884942

ACKNOWLEDGMENTS

I'd like to thank my whole family for always being there to support my ideas and decisions in life. Without my family, I don't know where'd I'd be. I'm very grateful to have you all.

CONTENTS

INTRODUCTION

Everyone will not make it in the music business. I've worked with some very talented musicians, who also happened to be horrible at business. In order to make it in the music industry, you will need to be musically astute and have an idea of how the music business works, inside and out. Behind the lyrics and melodies that you hear on the radio, TV, movies, Spotify, etc., there are record labels, investors, managers, lawyers, marketers, advisors, producers, videographers, directors, editors, sound engineers, publishers, and the list goes on. Talent or your good looks will only get you so far in the music business. In order to be truly successful you will need to master the various aspects of the business.

My goal in this book is to give you an understanding of the different aspects and roles within the music business, and to teach you how to use everyone playing these roles, to your full advantage. I will give you a hands-on perspective of what you will need to do to succeed. I will also reveal the moves I made, which led to selling millions of records and being awarded four RIAA plaques, a Grammy Award, ASCAP Award and YouTube Creator Award. I will also reveal secrets to some of my viral campaigns, which became huge successes.

I was born into the music business and as early as 10-years-old, I honestly never envisioned myself working far outside of the music and entertainment industry. I've learned from some of the best in the music business and I've also had success on an independent and major scale.

I had a head start in the music business and I was very fortunate to have my two uncles in my life, who are music industry veterans. My uncles were also good friends with guitar legend, Jimi Hendrix, and they have played just about every role, in the music business. My uncles were part of several bands throughout the 60s, 70s & 80s and also had their own music group, in which they were signed to a major label. They then became heads of their own record label, which was responsible for releasing some of Hip-Hop's earliest records. My uncles also owned a recording studio, in Times Square on 47th St in Manhattan, where Wu-Tang Clan recorded songs for their first album "Enter the Wu-Tang (36 Chambers)". At the time, Sean "Puff Daddy" Combs worked across the street, for Andre Harrell at Uptown/MCA Records, before he started Bad Boy Records, in 1993. My uncles mentored Andre Harrell.

From an early age, I've watched musicians' come and go. In this book, I will do my best to give you as much knowledge on how I was able to turn an unknown artist, into a Platinum selling and Grammy Nominated musician, in under three years. My goal in writing this book isn't to promise you success, in the music business. One thing I can guarantee, is that you will see results if you take some of the advice that I give in this book. Another goal is to save you time and energy, with hopes that you don't have to go through some of the downfalls that I have encountered. Persistence often surpasses natural talent. With the right equipment and know how, you can make it in the music & entertainment business. I hope this book becomes one of your many tools for success.

I have been planning on writing a book for almost 10 years now. I was unsure of what I would write my first book about. I decided to write a book on what I feel I'm most knowledgeable at… the music business. I study the music business day in and day out. I check the iTunes & Spotify charts, daily, for trends, new artists on the rise, and for general research purposes. To win in the streaming music age, you must be aware of the current trends. The music business is constantly changing. This book will give you a fresh perspective of the climate in which the music business is in right now in 2018, and the best way to succeed, in the least amount of time and hopefully, the least amount of effort. Seeking knowledge is a never-ending quest and I hope that you can use this book on your path to success.

In 2011, I officially signed my first artist to a management agreement. By 2013, I secured my artist a co-publishing deal with top producer Mike Will Made-It and Warner/Chappell. By 2014, there was a record label bidding war for my artist, which ended in him signing a multi-million dollar, major recording contract, with multi-platinum and multi Grammy Winning artist Drake and his OVO/Warner Brothers Record label.

What happened after that is the sad part of the story.

By writing this book, and sharing the information, I would hope you never have to go through, what I had to go through, in the music business.

This book is dedicated to my uncle Tunde-Ra Aleem. Thanks for everything you taught me. I think about you all the time. Rest in Paradise.

1 WHY DO YOU WANT TO BE IN THE MUSIC BUSINESS?

Why do you want to be in the music business? You really have to ask yourself this question before you get involved with the music industry. Are you in it for the money? Are you seeking fame? Do you really believe you have something good, that people honestly want to hear? Are you doing it because you think it seems cool? Are you a fan of music, and you'd like to be amongst other great musicians? Is this really your passion? Are you just a fan boy/girl who wants to be in the entertainment industry mix? What is your goal? Is your goal to sell a million or more records? Is your goal, simply to be famous, and prove to everyone in your town/city, that you have what it takes? Are you trying to prove to yourself, that you have what it takes? Are you trying to prove something to your family? What role will you be playing? Are you the artist? A producer? Are you a manager? Are you a publisher? Are you a record label? Are you an investor? Do you even know what any of that means? Maybe you are one of these. Maybe you are all of them. Maybe you are none of them. It's up to you, to find your way in this business. The first step is figuring out what your personal goals are, within the music business. You must be 100% clear on why you decided to venture in the music business, in the first place. It will save you a lot of time and headache. There are enough people floating aimlessly in the music business. You don't want to be one of those people... or do you? You have to decide that for yourself. If you are getting in the music business simply for the financial possibilities, then I'd suggest doing something else with your time. The music business can be very rewarding, but if it's only money that you seek, there are a lot of other ways to make money. The amount of unsuccessful people in the music business, far outweigh the amount that are successful, but don't let that discourage you.   My personal start in the music business happened indirectly. I started off as a videographer and my goal was to make films and television shows. In 2003, I began making short comedy videos with my brother's Sony Mini DV camcorder. I learned to edit videos and author DVDs and by 2004, I had a public access show that aired in Brooklyn, Manhattan, Staten Island and Portland, Maine. One day, my uncles were having a meeting, at our home in Brooklyn, with Dasun, a well-known writer based out of New York City. Another creative guy named Chris accompanied Dasun, during the meeting. Chris happened to be a fan of my public access show and soon joined our production team as an actor in the public access series. In 2006, I started to lose passion for the comedy public access show. In early 2007, I came up with the idea to make a documentary called "Criminals Gone Wild", which went extremely viral and landed me on Fox News, being interviewed by Bill O'Reilly and Geraldo Rivera. I told Chris that I wanted him to play a role in Criminals Gone Wild. Chris acted in the movie and introduced me to his buddy from Alabama, whom he recently started a rap group with. They both did an excellent job acting in the movie and Chris even found more of his acquaintances from his neighborhood in the Flatbush section of Brooklyn, to act in the film. I just purchased a Panasonic 100B Mini DV camera, and I was anxious to use the camera and learn as much as I could about video editing and the cameras various functions. At the time, Chris and his partner just released a mixtape and in exchange for helping me with my movie, I told Chris and his partner that I'd shoot some music videos for them, free of charge. I was starting to get better at editing and cutting their music videos sharpened my editing skills even more. These would be the first music videos that I had ever shot and edited during my career as a videographer. Since then, I have shot and edited over 60 music videos. At the time, I didn't realize it, but this would also be the beginning of my career as an artist manager.

2 BE A JACK-OF-ALL-TRADES

If you have the budget to hire people to do high quality work for you, then that's great. If you're starting your business with minimal amounts of funds, then I would recommend learning the skills that I will point out in this book. You will also need to learn to barter services with other creative people who may be able to help you in your journey.

It is now 2018 and a laptop is all you need to be a full-fledged force within the music business. I cannot put a value on the Apple MacBook Pro laptops, I have owned over the years. They were all priceless to me. The laptop I'm using to type this book, helped get me nominated for a Grammy Award.

In 1997, when I was 14, my father bought me my first desktop computer… a Gateway 2000. Probably the best gift my father ever bought me. I learned how to create websites using a program called Microsoft FrontPage. I learned how to read and write raw HTML (hypertext-markup language) code, while editing my websites. Websites need graphics, so I had to also learn Adobe Photoshop.

Learning how to create websites and knowing how to use Photoshop, are probably two of the most important skills that I learned early on. If you are an artist, start-up record label, manager, etc., you will need a graphic designer, very often. You probably wont make it far in the music business, if you don't learn basic Adobe Photoshop. Even if you aren't artistically inclined, you need to know how to function Photoshop. Go online and download free fonts. You can download as many fonts as your computer will store. Experiment with Photoshop. Learn how to place text on images. Learn to edit images and erase backgrounds. Learn about layers and typography. Know the difference between a .JPEG, .GIF, .PNG, .PSD, .PDF and .AI file. Study other graphic designers and emulate as much as possible.

If you don't want to learn Photoshop, then expect to be paying a graphic designer at least $25 to $100, every time you need some basic graphic design work done. You will need an in-house graphic designer, or someone easily accessible, who works directly with you, who can give you fast a turn around (less than 48 hours), and has a great eye for design. Usually, good graphic designers cost. If you can afford it, I'd recommend dribbble.com. Dribbble is a website where some of the best graphic designers in the world, showcase their work. You can then reach out to whichever graphic designer you choose and get a quote for your project. A nice logo, from a skilled graphic designer could cost you anywhere between $400 to $1000 dollars. If you'd like to go the cheap route, I'd recommend a site called fiverr.com. You can hire graphic designers for as little as $5 to $20 dollars. The quality of work will definitely not be as good as the designers from Dribbble, but if you have no graphic design skills and you'd like to get your project started as soon as possible, with minimum funds, Fiverr is a great resource. You can also use Fiverr and Dribbble to find website creators, app developers, video editors and pretty much any creative work, that you can think of.

When I'm developing a new artist, I create several social media profiles on sites such as Twitter, Instagram, Facebook, YouTube, Soundcloud, Pinterest, Tumblr, Blogger, Wordpress, Spotify, etc.. Each of these social media pages will need special sized graphics. I will talk more about each of these social media sites, and their advantages, later. YouTube page headers are supposed to be 2560x1440. Facebook and Twitter headers are a different size. Do you know how to format your images so that they will fit in the header space? Do you have a logo for your artist or brand? Did you or your artist do any photo shoots yet? Do you have a camera? Do you know how to use it? These are all things that you need to ask yourself.

Again, you can hire a photographer, for around $50 dollars an hour, or whatever the current going rate is for a photographer. If the key is to save money, then you need to be shooting your own photos. If you plan on building a record label or managing an artist, always be ready to take pictures. Know how to use your camera. If you're using your cell phone to take video, know NOT to shoot vertically. I've actually shot several decent quality impromptu music videos using only an iPhone. You really don't need much nowadays. The true essence of being creative is to create magic, with minimal resources. You ever notice how when an underground artist becomes mainstream, their music and videos stop being as good as they used to be? In my opinion, that's because people often allow money to get in the way of their creativity. Some artists get famous and make a lot of money, and then they fall off. Some people think their cash will make their productions better, but it usually makes it worse. When you feel as if you can throw money at a problem, then it's not really a problem. But when you have a real issue, and there's no money, you tend to find a way. Money can help make amazing things happen, but never let lack of money be an excuse for lack of production. The key to the music business nowadays is to stay relevant and release as much content, at a steady pace.

If you do hire a photographer, make sure to have a work-for-hire agreement that states that you have full ownership of the photos taken. You don't want anyone else capitalizing off your brand besides you and your partners. Any work that you hire an outside company to do, make sure you have them sign a "work-for-hire agreement". You can search "work for hire agreement" on any search engine, and you should be able to print a boilerplate agreement. The goal of the agreement is so that you own the rights to the photos (or graphics), and the photographer cannot exploit the photos without your consent. Always be in control of ALL of your intellectual property. A work for hire agreement ensures that you own all the rights to any work you paid an outside source to perform.

There are several platforms in which you can create a free website. I'd recommend using Blogger or Wordpress. Blogger and Wordpress are two blog platforms. If you don't know what a blog is, a blog is an online journal. It's a website in which you can frequently post content on, with minimal effort. Wordpress and Blogger are both free, but you will need to pay for your own domain name if you would like your website to be something like newartist.com. If you don't purchase your own domain, then your website address will look like this: newartist.blogspot.com or newartist.wordpress.com. Spend time learning how to customize your blog so that it fits your needs. Try out the different template styles and find one that fits your brand. I like to use the most basic templates. I don't like the newer templates that don't have regular scroll down navigation. I like to keep things as simple as possible for the viewer. Internet audience is very fickle and people's attentions spans nowadays are worse than ever. It's important that you get your message across fast. The goal is for your viewers to consume your content with simplicity and ease. No one wants to be searching around a website that they are not familiar with. People will simply just leave your website, if it's too complicated to navigate. Keep things as simple as possible. Put most of your emphasis on adding content to your website and making original graphics that coincide with your current campaign.

Continuity is also important. I always like it when I go to an artist's webpage, then I go to their Twitter or Facebook page, and all the graphics match. When you do this, it appears as if your brand has some structure. It also looks very professional. You don't want a different profile picture on each social media page. You are trying to leave lasting impressions in people's minds. Continuity and professionalism go hand and hand. Most major brands will keep their graphics the same across all social media pages and websites. Study other major brands and artist's social media pages and websites. Study their layouts, the design, what they have in bold, where the lettering is placed. In most instances, feel free to copy design ideas from major brands. Don't be afraid to emulate until you find your own path. The great artist Pablo Picasso is widely quoted as having said that "good artists borrow, great artists steal." I call it emulating. Remember, there is no new idea under the sun. So never feel bad for being inspired by someone else's work. When you reach a certain level, other people will start to emulate your work, and that's just the way it goes.

If you want your blog to look professional, you will need a header image. Again, you will need a graphic designer or know how to use Photoshop. Post as much content and information about yourself, your company, links to your social media pages, your music, your videos, photos, interviews, or any other content that you have, on this blog website that you create. You need to be updating your website, with new content, as much as possible. When you constantly release new content people will discover your brand organically. Having a website is key in being a part of the digital media age. If your brand doesn't have a website, then you better get one soon. Having your own website/blog should be on the top of your to-do list. A website is similar to having a storefront. People are accustomed to buying products from brands with a storefront. A website helps to ensure people that you are in business and serious about your e-commerce.

Buy a DSLR camera. The Canon 7D and the Canon 5D are two good DSLR cameras that a lot of creators use, to shoot videos and take photos. I purchased a 7D in 2012, and have been using it ever since. These particular cameras allow you to purchase interchangeable lenses, for desired visual effect. I didn't bother upgrading to an expensive lens. I kept the basic standard lens on my camera and I was always able to take excellent pictures and shoot great quality video footage. I've been hearing a lot of good things about a new camera called the Panasonic Lumix GH5. This is a new camera that was just released in May 2017 and it shoots 4K video. I plan on purchasing a GH5 soon.

If you are a label, artist, manager, producer, etc., it's really good to have your own camera. Never solely depend on other people to shoot or create your content. You must take a proactive stance if you want to succeed. The DSLR cameras are really easy to use and come with presets, so you don't really need to go to photography or film school to get up and running. I recommend that you study your camera and watch as many video as you can about whichever particular camera you choose, in order to get the best results.

Content is key. Shoot as much footage and take as many pictures as you can. Learn to edit your footage. Learn to edit your photos. I started out editing video on Adobe Premiere using my PC. I then graduated to a MacBook Pro and started editing on Final Cut Pro. Learn how to use Final Cut, Adobe Premiere or any editing software that you feel comfortable with, as soon as possible. Also learn the best formats to convert your video footage, for Internet viewing. You want to be uploading high bitrate h264 mp4 videos to YouTube and other online video platforms. Learn about "Internet video conversion". Learn to convert your videos to even sizes for platforms like Instagram and know how to convert to a perfect square such as 640x640 while retaining aspect ratio with letterbox.

Final Cut and most editing programs allow you to import .PSD and other image formats from Photoshop. This is another reason you need to learn how to use Photoshop. You will need to create graphics for your video productions, when needed also. I cannot stress how important Photoshop is. I have also used Photoshop to create one-sheet presentations. I never like to go to a business meeting without at least a one sheet or an executive summary. I usually design my one sheet in Photoshop, then have it printed at Kinkos on card stock, then get the sheet coil bound with a transparent cover, and black back, so that my one sheet looks like a one page book. It's always professional when you have a presentation to leave with whomever you are meeting with. Most times, people rarely remember exactly what was said in a meeting. The one sheet should help remind the person you met, exactly what the dialog was, during the meeting.

I also had to learn how to be a sound engineer so that I could record audio professionally, using Avid Pro Tools software. I am far from an expert and I eventually would like to learn more about sound engineering and mixing & mastering audio. I've been tightening my sound engineering skills on Pro Tools for the past 7 years. I still have a lot to learn and haven't taken any formal classes yet. In the music industry, good sound engineers are always needed and highly respected. If properly using the latest audio plug-ins, good sound engineers can turn the worst singer into a decent sounding singer, using vocal tuning software. Again, if you can afford it, go ahead and spend $1000 to $2500 a day recording your songs (or your artist's) songs at the best recording studios. Realistically, you need to be recording at home, to perfect your songs, before you go to a professional recording studio. "Reference tracks" are rough versions of a song that one may record at home, prior to working with a professional engineer or producer who may help to make the song sound a lot better. Record a rough version of your song, and practice it, before you commit to an expensive studio session, with an pro engineer. Don't get too caught up in the quality of your reference songs. The goal of the reference song is to get the idea from out of your head and onto a recording. You should learn to be proficient in Pro Tools or Logic to record your reference songs. If you do not have Pro Tools, use any audio recording software that you can find, to record your reference songs. The main issues to worry about when recording, is making sure there isn't much background noise, and making sure the microphone levels are good so that your audio is not peaking.

Before we recorded our songs with professional sound engineers, we recorded the songs ourselves, using an AKG 420 Condenser Mic. You don't want to waste anyone's time at the studio, especially your own time... and dime. It's best to experiment at home (or wherever you record), and then when you go to a real sound studio with a professional engineer, you'll be ready and know exactly how you want the finished product to sound.

You don't necessarily need to be in an expensive studio, to get radio ready songs. My first platinum song was recorded in a bedroom at Metro Boomin's home. Metro Boomin is now one of the top producers in the music business and I was fortunate to work with him. Metro had a great in-house sound engineer named Justin Childs, working at his townhouse, when we recorded our songs. Prior to working with Metro and Justin, we recorded countless reference songs, on our own.

This is the music business. At the very least, you will need a graphic designer, a videographer, an editor, a sound engineer, a songwriter, a producer, a web designer, recording software and a decent microphone. It's in your best interest to be a jack of all of these trades that I mentioned. These are the main skills and tools needed to deliver an award winning and chart topping music project. If you can make it past this step, and deliver a finished product, you are on your way to being on the Billboard charts! You are now your own record label, if you possess the skills to deliver a finished song, ready for distribution. Now you're ready to sell your song. You're going to need an LLC so that you can cash those music checks that will be coming in soon! I'll explain why you should set up an LLC in the next chapter.

3 STARTING AN LLC

You will need to create a business so that you can accept checks from clients, in the business's name. You will also need to pay the proper state and federal income taxes, on every sale that you make through your business. The purpose of setting up an LLC, is to protect you from personal liability caused by business. This means that members are not personally liable for debts and court judgments incurred by the LLC. Creditors are unable to seek the personal assets of the LLCs members. For example, if you were performing at a show, and a riot took place at the venue you were performing, and several people got injured, you can be personally sued. Under the LLC, the claimant can only sue for the business's assets and not your personal assets. So you wont have to worry about losing the cash you have saved in your personal savings or checking account. There are different business structures that you can choose. The business structure you choose will have legal and tax implications. Learn about the different types of business structures and find the one best suited for your business. I have always set up LLCs for all of my music and entertainment ventures. An LLC blends certain positive attributes of a sole proprietorship, partnership, and corporation without some of the drawbacks of these organizations. Each state has different filing rules, when setting up your LLC. Most states allow you to file online. Some states allow you to pay the fee online, and then you can print a .PDF file of your business certificate instantly. Fees can range anywhere between $100-400, to set up an LLC in the state of your choice. After you set up your LLC, you will need an EIN number from the IRS. You can file for an EIN number online, for free, at www.irs.gov/businesses. Once you have your LLC certificate and EIN number, you can go to any bank and open up a business account. Now that you are a business owner, you will need to remember to keep a log of every business transaction that you make. This is called "bookkeeping". If you spend money on anything, make sure to write it down. If money comes in, write it down. Bookkeeping is all about having several documented records of the financial transactions of a business. The bookkeeping should be easy to read and accessible by all partners of the business, in all fairness. You will also need to report your income and expenses to the IRS, so make sure to keep good track of your financial records. I like to keep all receipts, even thought I have every business debit card transaction documented in my online banking account. Keep track of the business money and only spend the LLC income, to reinvest back into the business. If you get in the habit of spending the profits made from your new LLC, then your business will stagnate. Pay people when necessary and save money whenever and wherever possible. There are also several tax benefits when you are a business owner. Most daily business expenses, such as travel, business lunches, business vehicle, business phone line, etc., are eligible for tax write offs, which means you will get money back from the government on some of the taxes that you may have paid. It would be wise to speak with an accountant or tax advisor, when business starts to pick up. Small business loans are also another advantage of having an LLC. If you have established good credit, you may be eligible for business startup capital from a bank. Forming an LLC may help a new business establish credibility with potential customers, employees, vendors and partners because they see you have made a formal commitment to your business.

4 DIGITAL DISTRIBUTION (GETTING YOUR MUSIC ON SPOTIFY, ITUNES, ETC.)

Next I will explain to you how I got my start with digital distribution of music. Digital distribution (also called content delivery, online distribution) is the delivery or distribution of media content such as audio and video.

During the first months of working with Chris and his partner, I shot and edited 5 music videos for them. At the time, rapper Soulja Boy was at his peak with his hit song "Crank That Soulja Boy". Chris's group made two remixes of Soulja Boy's #1 hit song called "Crank That Spiderman" and "Crank That Batman" and then I accompanied the songs with music videos. Since "Crank That Soulja Boy" was the top song at the time, everyone was searching for anything "Crank That" related, which led people to finding the "Crank That Spiderman" song & video. To this day, the "Crank That Spiderman" video I shot has received over 11 million views on YouTube. This was my first music video that went viral. Chris had a friend who had a home studio in Connecticut, so we left Brooklyn and headed to Hartford to work at Chris's friend's studio. While we were there, I started to do management work for Chris's rap group. By the way, his rap group name was called "Duffle Bag Boiz". I applied all of the skills that I practiced from Chapter 2 to help set up Duffle Bag Boiz online presence. At the time MySpace was the biggest social media site. I set up official websites for DBB and even set them up a video podcast in the iTunes Store. Setting up a podcast is pretty easy; all you need to do is learn to set up an .XML feed, in the proper formats for iTunes to read, then upload

12

your .XML feed to an accessible internet server. The Duffle Bag Boiz iTunes podcast shot to #1 in no time! I made two separate podcasts for them. One podcast was set up for their "Crank That" songs and videos, and another for their new mixtape that they released, which had the "Crank That" songs on it as well.

Due to Soulja Boy's popularity at the time, Duffle Bag Boiz were getting hundreds of thousands of streams, downloads, and new fans. It was amazing! Our timing played a major role in the success of the podcasts. At the time, I didn't know how to deliver music for sale on iTunes, and this was when the concept of "streaming music" was still new to most people. Had I known how to deliver music to iTunes for paid download, we would have gotten rich overnight, due to Soulja Boy's extreme buzz at the time, and us having a remix available to his overly popular #1 song and dance. The podcast kept dominating the iTunes Podcast section and the major labels started questioning our marketing tactics. Interscope kept removing the podcast claiming that we were infringing on their copyrights, which wasn't true, because we remade the "Crank That" instrumental and we didn't use any of their master recordings. The sounds used on the "Crank That Soulja Boy" song were so simple, you couldn't tell the difference from a remake or the original.

Soon we were getting calls from different record labels, interested in meeting Duffle Bag Boiz. We were surely ahead of our time. At this time, most people didn't even know what a podcast was. This was around the time indie labels were still selling CDs out the trunks of cars. One day in Hartford, while doing online research, I stumbled on an article about a new service called "Tunecore", that allowed you to sell your music videos on iTunes. I had been trying to sell my short comedy videos from my public access show on iTunes for years, but the only way in the iTunes store, for an indie video creator like myself, was through the free iTunes Podcast Store. I was forced to learn about RSS (Rich Site Summary or Really Simple Syndication) and I learned how to write .XML feeds, while trying to promote my comedy series, by any means. The podcast creation knowledge helped me a lot with the Duffle Bag Boiz project, as well as projects that I'm involved with to this day. I was easily able to learn how to create .XML feeds due to me already understanding and having a knowledge writing HTML code, which is very similar.

This is when I realized music had the power to reach people, way faster than film. I started to realize the viral power of music, and how music spreads fast from one ear to another. I had tons of short comedy videos to market online, but I never had an original music project to market before the Duffle Bag Boiz project. This experience was priceless and really groomed me for my future career as an artist manager and record producer.

At the time, Tunecore charged about $275 to encode and upload a music video to the iTunes Store, for $1.99 per download. I paid Tunecore the $550 for "Crank That Spiderman" & "Crank That Batman" video to appear in the iTunes Store. I waited weeks for the videos to appear, until I totally forgot about it.

In between working with Duffle Bag Boiz on everything from writing and producing new music, marketing ideas, promotion and planning, I spent my spare time, editing the Criminals Gone Wild footage. I was able to get some great footage in Connecticut, and the time I spent there was beneficial in the completion of the film. At the time, I was just going with the flow, but as I reflect, I'm really glad I had the opportunity to go to Connecticut with the Duffle Bag Boiz. The situation was working itself out. A month or so went by and we were planning our next move. I finished a trailer for Criminals Gone Wild and released it online. Lots of websites reposted the trailer due to the shocking material that they witnessed. The trailer was really starting to buzz and I was starting to put more time and effort into promoting the CGW movie, than I was with the Duffle Bag Boiz project. I was also starting to have personal differences with Chris's rap partner in the Duffle Bag Boiz group. I felt as if Chris's partner was selfish and self-centered and we had no contractual obligation to work together, so I left Connecticut before the situation got too uncomfortable, and continued my path promoting Criminals Gone Wild. Chris was upset, because we were really starting to make progress. I didn't want any of us to get into an altercation, so I left Hartford to continue promoting my new movie. Criminals Gone Wild ended up becoming a huge marketing success and next thing I knew, I was on every television news network being interviewed about the film.

Fast forward to Spring 2008, I was back in Brooklyn about to head to Chicago to do an assignment for The History Channel. A production company, who produced the TV show "Gangland", was seeking footage about Chicago gang culture. While I was in Brooklyn, planning my trip to Chicago, it dawned on me that I sent the Duffle Bag Boiz videos to iTunes over 6 months ago. "There had to be some money in that Tunecore account by now", is what I thought. The "Crank That Spiderman" video was rejected because of a glitch in the video, but the "Crank That Batman" video had made its way in the iTunes Store for sale. I totally forgot about it, until I logged in the Tunecore account and seen over $2000 dollars waiting for me to withdraw! It blew my mind, because I had never made that much money, from uploading content on the Internet. It really blew my mind and I was amazed! The light bulbs started blinking in my head and I realized if I could make $2000 in a month with one video… I imagined how much I could make with 5 videos, 10 videos, or 20 videos on iTunes. I was really on to something, yet, still oblivious of the money we could have been making, simply by selling our songs on iTunes, instead of music videos, which take longer to process and produce.

I immediately told my brother AliAta and my cousin Sulaiman about my iTunes success story. At that point, I no longer was interested in working with the Duffle Bag Boiz. I felt as if they were ungrateful for the work that I had done for them. Chris had also started a smear campaign against me, while Criminals Gone Wild was circulating in the media. Due to the smear campaign, I did not want to help DBB anymore, but I knew I needed a rap group as soon as possible, so that I could see exactly how much money I could make, remixing popular songs and sending them to iTunes for sale.

At the time, 50 Cent and his group G-Unit were hot, and so was Soulja Boy.

SOULJA UNIT was born. Sulaiman, and me met up with our producer partner Supremo Massiv (who is now in a rock band called Revel In Dimes) and recorded a song called "iDance". At the time, Soulja Boy was planning for his second album and he was trying to decide on his first single. Right after Soulja Boy announced that "iDance" would be the name of his new single, we were in the studio recording our version of "iDance". The next day, my brother helped us shoot a video for the "iDance" song. I went home and edited the video and then I sent the song and video to iTunes, using Tunecore again. The next day we went back to Supremo's studio and sped the tempo up on the "iDance" instrumental and recorded an "iDance (Remix)" with new lyrics. My brother AliAta wrote a verse on "iDance (Remix)" and joined the Soulja Unit group with the two of us. We shot a video for that song the next day also. We then sent that single to iTunes as well. We continued remaking songs that we predicted would be future hits, but weren't yet for sale, by the original artist, in the iTunes store. In the weeks to come, we continued to release several songs and videos. Our first payment finally came from Tunecore, for the Soulja Unit songs, 45 days after that initial month was over. Soulja Unit made over $6500 that month in digital downloads and streams! Up until that day, I had never made that much money in one month. The Soulja Unit project was a success and my life changed forever. I was finally making real money, for my creative work and it was all because of digital distribution!

We continued to predict hit songs and the Soulja Unit project eventually would earn us over $300,000 in royalties over the next 365 days! It was a real life changer. I was able to buy my first luxury car, in cash, which was a Mercedes-Benz CLK430. I had modest goals at the time and all I really wanted was to have a nice car and decent income. My grandma passed away and I moved into her old house in Akron, Ohio, since the mortgage was paid off and I could live rent-free. I built a home studio at my grandma's house using the proceeds from the iTunes sales.

Eminem was about to release his new album "Relapse" and announced that the first song would be called "Crack A Bottle". Before Interscope could release "Crack A Bottle" for sale, Soulja Unit had the "Crack A Bottle (Remix)" posted on iTunes. We did over 25,000 downloads of "Crack A Bottle", in a few days, before Interscope caught wind and sent Tunecore & iTunes a cease & desist takedown notice. We technically weren't in the wrong because we did not use Eminem's beat, nor did we use any of his lyrics other than us chanting a similar hook. Our version was a parody of his song, and free speech laws protect parodies. Unfortunately, Interscope didn't think our parody was funny and they did everything they could to stop the Soulja Unit operation. At the time, Soulja Boy, 50 Cent and Eminem were all signed to Interscope, so they were pissed that we were making a name for ourselves, and making money, while riding their waves. The major labels hate this kind of activity and they threatened Soulja Unit with several takedown notices. It was the beginning of the end for Soulja

Unit project.

The major labels were bullying us because we were playing by our own rules and I even started to get familiar with legal loopholes that protect parody and cover song artists. We didn't use Eminem's image or likeness on the cover art, nor did we sample Interscope's master recordings of "Crack A Bottle". I spoke with Tunecore founder Jeff Price about the major label harassment and he told me that there wasn't much that he could do to protect the artist using his Tunecore service. Jeff Price later left Tunecore after he sold his shares in the company. When Jeff left Tunecore, their policies started getting even worse. I personally don't use Tunecore to this day. Whenever I would make substantial amounts of money on Tunecore, they would freeze my account. To me, Tunecore became more like Internet police than digital music distributors. The same goes for Songcast (another digital distribution service). I have an even worse opinion about Songcast. The owner once kept more than $10,000 from me, because he didn't agree with my marketing tactics, even though all of the songs I sold, were original songs, that we created from scratch. The owner of Songcast froze my account, took my money and then argued to me that I was misleading people on iTunes. That's an argument that he could never prove, nor did it state anywhere in the Songcast terms of service that my activity wasn't approved. I don't doubt that some people were misled by our music. I buy things all the time that I may end up not liking later. Other times, I've bought items that I grew appreciation for. The fact is, people find and enjoy new and different music all the time, and $0.99 is a small price to pay for any level of creativity. So for him to say that I was misleading people, when in fact, all I was doing was marketing my creativity, I feel that he was wrong. With that being said, I've never downloaded any song unconsciously. iTunes even gives you the choice to preview a song before buying it. This was not some scam, and I was selling music legally, yet the owner of Songcast took it upon himself to make judgment upon my marketing methods and kept all of the money that I made that month. Combined, Songcast and Tunecore have taken tens of thousands of dollars from several of my accounts, all because they didn't agree with my music marketing methods, at the time. It started to seem like the digital distributors, who claim they work in favor of the indies, were actually working on behalf of the major labels.

The Internet was like the Wild West for a while and now that a few online business owners are making tons of money, they are taking it upon themselves to dictate what activity is right or wrong on the Internet, despite if you are abiding by all legal parameters. These people who I usually refer to as "trolls", feel as if they have the right to dictate what happens on the Internet. Most artists who use these digital distribution services will never make more than $100 on any given month, so when they see someone cashing out thousands every month, it raises a red flag in their minds that you are doing something wrong. You'd think Songcast would embrace your monetary success, but instead, they looked for an excuse to take my money. I can only imagine what the owner bought for himself with the extra $10,000+ dollars he pocketed from my music sales. Some people just don't like to see others winning.

At the time, MP3 downloads and streaming was a new thing, and everyone, indie and major, were trying to adjust and find their way in. I did what I had to do to make money and learn as much as I could about digital distribution and the music business. Unfortunately, Tunecore and Songcast didn't agree with my methods and they decided to pocket my hard earned money. Again, I do not recommend either of these services.

With the "Crack A Bottle" money, my cousin Sulaiman was able to purchase himself a new MacBook Pro and he left New York, to come to Ohio with me to work on more music. We knew we would have to change our group name, so we came up with the name "Good Ol' American Boys". We made a bunch of songs under "GOAB" and made good money. On a regular month, we were splitting anywhere from $6000-8000 dollars... sometimes more. These were good times for us. Soon, I caught wind of a new artist named Drake, who had just signed to Lil Wayne's record label, Young Money/Cash Money Records. We heard about his song "Successful", that was starting to buzz. I then learned about Compulsory Licenses.

It is not against the law to remake someone else's song, word-for-word. As long as you remake all elements of the song, such as the beat and you record the lyrics, with your own voice, you have the right to sell that song, after sending a Compulsory License, notifying the publishers of the song, of your planned usage of their lyrics and composition. Monopolies are illegal in the United States and it also applies to songs. Copyright law won't allow you to be the only person able to release a particular song. As long as the compulsory license user pays the publisher a fee of **9.1 cents** per download (which left us with $0.57, after iTunes took their 1/3 cut of a $0.99 song download). "Successful" was our biggest song at the time, and we made over $45,000 from it, by the time Drake came out with his official version. My cousin Sulaiman was able to buy his first car, a BMW 328i coupe, in cash. We kept making new songs that would sell and we continued to cash in.

Digital distribution had changed our lives. Never before could an indie artist have their songs available in one of the biggest marketplaces in the world. We didn't have to worry about pressing up costly CDs, having a major record deal with major distribution and any other stress and obligation that comes with a record deal. We were able to operate quietly out of my grandmother's old house, and make a decent living, selling our songs.

That's how I got my start with digital distribution. Digital distribution has empowered the music industry and all independent artists. Spotify streaming royalties now makes up for 73% of overall music royalties. A few years ago, downloads were dominant but in the past couple years, streaming has taken over. Your music will not be included in online streaming stores without a digital distributor. Lately, I have been using DistroKid, to distribute my music to the online digital/streaming music retailers.

Streaming royalties are also on the rise. Five years ago, streaming revenue was significantly lower than it is today. Now, artists are enjoying better streaming royalty rates. If you have music available, get your music digitally distributed to online music stores today. There is no reason that your music catalog should not be available for streaming or download.

Once your single, EP or album is ready, you can send your music to be digitally distributed using the distributor of your choice. You will need to convert your song files to whichever format they accept. Usually full quality .WAV files are acceptable. I use the iTunes app to convert audio files to the correct format for distribution. Next you will need album art. Your album art will need to be at least 1500x1500 in size. If your album art isn't that size, you can always resize your art in Photoshop. Once you upload your audio files and album artwork, there is a fee. Different distributors charge different amounts. DistroKid only charges annually and they have 3 different levels of membership. I wouldn't recommend any digital distributor that takes a cut of your royalties. CDBaby has been around for a while and I've had good experiences using their distribution service. The downside to CDBaby is that they take 9% of your digital royalties on every payment. CDBaby is a great service with excellent customer service, but I'd rather keep 100% of my royalties. There are several online digital distributors and you are free to use whichever one you feel most comfortable with.

There is no reason for you not to have your music in all of the digital music stores. If you have music, then it needs to be available for people to consume. If not, then you are wasting valuable time. Every stream counts, every download counts. It will all start to add up after a while. Before Makonnen got signed to OVO/Warner, I had already digitally distributed 10 albums of his music. We had a catalog of at least 100 songs, which I released, in less than three years. 8 of the 10 albums weren't studio quality, but I really didn't care. In my opinion, as long as it can be heard, then it's ready to go. People who get caught up in quality, usually put less music out. If you have the luxury to produce studio quality songs, then go ahead. If you are not able to afford mixing and mastering, then still put your music out for sale. I personally enjoy listening to rough sounding, grass-roots style music. It sounds more real to me.

I was a big fan of 50 Cent before he partnered with Eminem and Dr. Dre. A lot of 50 Cent's early mixtapes weren't produced with much emphasis on quality, yet, 50 released tons of mixtapes and his brand became big, without the help of a major label push. These countless mixtapes that 50 Cent released ended up catching the attention of Eminem, which led to his major label deal with Shady/Aftermath/Interscope. This was in the early era of digital distribution, before iTunes and Spotify became household names and I speak of actual physical mixtape CDs that 50 Cent was producing. Yet the method remains the same. Be prolific and release as much content as possible. Releasing your music in digital stores put you in the marketplace and people tend to take you more serious when you are releasing product for sale.

Good music promotes itself, so it's counterproductive to the growth of a music brand, if you are not releasing your music. Building a catalog of music for sale will pay off in the long run. Don't get too caught up in quality. Your music will get better as time goes by and fans will be able to hear the growth in your music. People are already used to hearing high quality music, because they play it all day on the radio. It can make you stand out when your music sounds rough around the edges. Don't take what I'm saying the wrong way. If you have the means to make the best quality music, then do so. My point is, do not let the fear of not being able to release high quality music, stop you from releasing your music. That is the worst mistake an artist or label can make. You must be prolific if you want to make it in the music business nowadays. Make yourself a contender by having your catalog available in the marketplace. No matter how good your music quality is, people may still listen to it and think it sucks. No matter how good your music sounds, you cannot control people's opinions. The goal is to find people who like your style of music and not worry whether people will discriminate on your music based on the quality. Most people don't know what they want until you give it to them, anyway. Make your music as available as possible by digitally distributing it.

Never before have artists had the ability to release their music so easily to the whole world, until recently. Prior to digital distribution, you had to actually get records, cassettes or CDs pressed up, which was a costly process. A nice portion of profit, used to go into the actual production of the physical product. That has all changed with digital distribution. Take advantage of the benefits of digital distribution and don't get too caught up in the quality or mix of your music. The most important thing to do is to maintain a quality brand. Music naturally gets better as you practice. If you don't put music out, then you're not practicing, you're stagnating.

5 ENTERTAINMENT LAWYERS

At some point, when your project starts to take off, you may need a lawyer to help you understand some of the contracts that may be coming your way. You don't really need a lawyer, and any information that you seek is an Internet search away, but if you have access to a good entertainment lawyer, then I'd recommend keeping one on speed dial. You better hope you have some sort of understanding with the lawyer also. Some lawyers will turn the clock on and charge you for every minute that you speak with them. Be very careful not to retain a lawyer's services until you can afford it, or it seems absolutely necessary. Some lawyers may talk with you for hours, while you're oblivious that their rate clock is on. Everyone is in the game to make money, just like you are and if you think a lawyer is giving you free information, either you're very lucky, or you better think twice. I was fortunate to know several entertainment lawyers that previously worked with my uncles. This is another reason why you never burn bridges and try to keep as many open relationships as possible. You may not be thinking this far ahead yet, but the people who you are doing business with now, your children may have to do business with them also. There are lots of people on the outside of the music business, but the inner circle of lawyers, labels reps, agents, managers, etc., is a very small circle of folks. You do not want to burn any bridges, with anyone in the industry. If you are doing bad business, word may get around fast and people may not want to work with you. The entertainment business is all about relationships. Being a manager, another thing I had to learn the hard way was, DO NOT introduce your artist to your lawyer! If you are an artist, it may be in your best interest to hire your own lawyer. If you are an artist with a manager or an artist signed to a label, it's not in your best interest to use the same lawyer your manager is using (or your label is using). This is called a "conflict of interest". Do as much research as possible on the term and be sure to stay clear of conflicts of your interest. Your only interest is to win. If three people are all fighting to win, someone will have to be the loser and most lawyers are happy to take the silver medal, if you know what I mean. In a perfect world, your lawyer will work for you and work for your artist and vice versa, and you will all work together with loyalty and harmony until the end of the business agreement. Realistically, things don't usually work out that way. It's a cutthroat business where there are often more losers than winners. You want to stay on the winning side, and one way to do that, is to have your own lawyer, that is protecting your interest and YOUR INTEREST ONLY! Remember, this business is all about YOU WINNING... and I say that with all due respect to your business partners. One of the biggest mistakes I made, was introducing my artist to my lawyer. Once I introduced my client to my lawyer, it marked the beginning of the end for my first artist management project, and I'll tell you why. When my project started to take off, and we started getting radio play, my lawyer started making suggestions to my artist. NO ONE should be making any suggestions to YOUR artist, besides you, as the manager. Your lawyer should make suggestions to you, on your behalf, but they should never be making suggestions to your client. This is called "tortious interference", also known as intentional interference with contractual relations. Tortious interference is when two people are working together under a contractual obligation, then a third party comes along and damages the business relationships with their actions or by making suggestions which could then alter the perception or thought process of the two people who were working together in the contractual agreement. This is a no no and that's why you should keep your lawyer, far away from your clients. Your artist never needs to meet your lawyer. If you are an artist, get your own lawyer. It may cost you now, but it will save you heartache later, when you realize the lawyer your label or manager, set you up with, is really working in the label or your manager's best interest... INSTEAD OF YOURS! If you've never watched the movie "Blow" starring Johnny Depp, you should check it out. It's a true story and an excellent movie that shows a perfect example of tortious interference in business. The film shows what could happen when you reveal your lawyer or your "connect" to your client. In the movie, a man named George Jung was a cocaine dealer. He was buying all of his cocaine from a guy named Diego, who worked for Pablo Escobar. Diego wanted to know how George was moving so much cocaine, but George never told Diego how. George knew a nightclub owner named Derek Foreal. Derek was able to move all of George's cocaine, which he got from Diego, but neither Diego nor Derek knew each other. George made the mistake of telling Diego that it was really Derek who was moving all the kilos of cocaine. Diego soon started working directly with Derek and the two cut George out of the cocaine deals. Unfortunately, George couldn't sue either of them, because they were all involved in the illegal drug trade. Fortunately, I was able to sue and I won my case. If I could have avoided it all, I would have. Do NOT introduce your clients to your lawyer! Your personal lawyer should be like an imaginary friend that no one sees but you. People talk a good one when they need your help, but the minute they get to where they need to be, they will treat you like you never mattered. Sad to say, money is the root of all evil and most people will stab their own mother in the back for the dream of millions of dollars and fame. Money shows people's true colors and you never really know who someone is until they have a substantial amount of money. One minute you're looking at someone like a brother or sister, the next day, they're your worst enemy. It's a really shady business. Protect yourself with the best contracts as possible. Make sure you are covered in every way possible and avoid conflicts of interest. Remember, your goals from Chapter One. Losing is not a part of this game I speak of. This book was made, to teach you how to win, not lose. I didn't get in this business to be ripped off, and neither should you. When you find a good lawyer, it is important that you tell him or her exactly what YOU want. The goal is for YOU to leave the business deal in the positive, not in the negative. The goal is for YOU to win and for you to avoid getting ripped off. I made the mistake of only planning for the positive, that I felt would eventually come, due to the hard work that I invested. I never took the time to consider the negative aspects of what could possibly happen later on down the line. Plan for the positive and also be prepared for worst-case scenarios. Most artists get so caught up in winning, that they totally disregard and forget the people who helped them get to the finish line. Make sure your contract states what you want out of your deal with your client. Again, it goes back to what I said in Chapter One. Know what you want. Know why you are in the business. Set goals. Know your goals. Complete your goals and make sure you don't get ripped off. Do not be naïve and always assume that people are out to get you. Never let your guard down. That doesn't mean you have to portray yourself in a defensive fashion. Just keep in mind that, what can happen, will happen. If you fail to plan, then you plan to fail. This may be some of the most important information that I share. Do not put yourself in a position to get ripped off. You will regret it deeply. This is probably one of the most important chapters in this book because if you get ripped off in the end of your project, it somewhat defeats the purpose in all of the other information in the book. I'm not in the business of getting ripped off and I would hope you aren't either. People will justify ripping you off by saying things like, "it's business, it's not personal", but that's nonsense if you ask me. It always becomes personal when you cannot feed your family due to someone being disloyal and running off with money that you are owed. I would hope that you wouldn't share your spouse with your business partners. Think of your lawyer the same way.

6 CONTRACTS & 360 DEALS

If you plan to succeed in the music business, you will need to learn how to read and understand the language of different types of contracts. Never rush to sign a contract. Before you sign a contract, you need to be 100% clear on what you are signing. Referring back to Chapter One, you need to know what your goals are, in the music business. Your goals should coincide with any contracts that you sign. Most people get so caught up in the allure of fast money and getting an advance, that they never truly read and understand their contracts. Don't be that person. Never feel like you were forced or rushed into signing any agreements. Your life, career, future and family could be on the line. Having an entertainment lawyer that is knowledgeable is very important. Your lawyer can help you to decipher contract jargon.

Never commit to work, on behalf of anyone, without some sort of written agreement or contract. If you are an artist, seeking a manager, be ready to sign some sort of management agreement. If you are interested in helping to further the career of a friend, family member, or someone creative, that you believe in, then you may be taking on the role of a manager, without realizing it. It's best to sign agreements with people before you commit to doing any work for them, even if you are friends or family. I've seen family members and best friends fall out over money and business differences. This happens because people often fail to create contractual agreements and fully take the time to create exact terms and definitions of their working relationships, early on.

Never rely on verbal or "hand-shake" agreements. Have your agreements in writing. It will be easier for you to avoid disputes if everything is already in writing. You don't necessarily need a lawyer, to draft a good contract that will hold up in court. The most important part about your contract should be that it's clear and concise. Search the Internet for contracts that suit your needs and feel free to change anything in the contract, that doesn't suit you. When writing your contract, know your goals and what you want to achieve from the business relationship, you are about to enter.

If you are the one receiving a contract to sign, you have the freedom to change anything in the contract that you don't agree with. Again, never feel forced to agree to anyone else's terms. Remember, this is your career and life. Don't be so quick to sign other people's contracts.

Recently, an artist that I know needed help furthering his career. He has a song that was featured on a well-known movie franchise soundtrack. I was attempting to help him retrieve some unpaid publishing royalties that he didn't know was owed to him. He didn't set up his own publishing company, therefore he had thousands of dollars of uncollected music royalties. I will speak more about publishing and setting up your own publishing company in Chapter 10. I was interested in managing him, yet I knew he was tied to some sort of contractual obligation with a Grammy winning producer that he works with. I asked to see his contract so that I could figure out where I fit into the equation. I definitely don't like stepping on other people's toes (meaning I wouldn't try to manage an artist who is already in a management agreement) and I needed to read his contract before I decided exactly what our next steps would be. He was oblivious as to what sort of contract he signed. He didn't know whether he signed a publishing agreement, a recording agreement or a management agreement. The only thing he knew was, he got paid $7500 to sign it. I couldn't do anything to help him until I knew exactly what his contract stated. Six months went by and he still didn't deliver his contract to me. He didn't even know where his contract was. Don't be this type of person. Don't get so caught up in money, that you sign away your life in business obligations. In the end, when the advance money for signing runs out, you will become bitter and ultimately start looking for a way out of the contract, which can lead to you being sued for breach of contract. Nobody wants to be sued. It's very costly to hire a lawyer to defend a lawsuit, especially when you are in the wrong. I'm sure no lawyer wants to fight a case that they're sure to lose, and the legal expenses to fight a losing case, will come out of your pocket.

I recently won a lawsuit due to an artist I was managing, breaching our agreement. I was able to find a great lawyer to work my case pro-bono. *Pro bono* publico (English: for the public good; usually shortened to *pro bono*) is a Latin phrase for professional work undertaken voluntarily and without payment. The only reason I was able to find a lawyer to work on my breach of management agreement case without paying upfront lawyer fees was because of my contract. If I didn't have the contract, then it would have been a lot harder to convince a lawyer to take my case, without an upfront payment.

Lawyers have a saying, "contracts are meant to be broken". That's bullshit if you ask me. Be honorable. If you agree to work with someone and decide to do a contract together, do your best to fulfill your end of the agreement. Have integrity. Don't be the one to breach the contract. Leave that for someone else. Your contract is there to protect you incase the other party breaches the agreement you signed together. In that case, you can sue to recover any losses that you incurred. Lawsuits are very stressful and they cause anguish. Be honorable, fulfill your end of the contract, and before you know it, your contract period will be over. You can continue to be business partners or friends with the other party, after the contract is over, if you choose, or you can go your separate ways. That is how good business is done.

People who enter the entertainment industry, and ultimately burn bridges with the people, who help them, don't make it far in the industry. Be honorable. Being honorable is just as important as making good music. If word gets around that you aren't a man or woman of your word, then very few people will want to deal with you and it may hinder your career in the long run.

When someone is looking to breach a contract, they will find any excuse to get out of the contract, so make sure you are fulfilling your end of the agreement, to the fullest. If you don't want to fulfill your end of the agreement to the fullest, then DON'T SIGN A CONTRACT!

Always scan or take photos of your contracts, for digital safe keeping. There are several free phone apps that I use to scan documents, such as "Genius Scan" and "Tiny Scanner". Usually after signing an agreement, I will take a picture of the document, using Genius Scan, and then I will email the agreement to myself. That way, if the original contract is lost, destroyed, or damaged, you will still have a digital version to retrieve in the future.

Know what type of contract you are signing. I'm currently mediating a situation where an artist I'm representing doesn't know whether he signed a recording agreement or a co-publishing agreement, or both. I requested that his publisher send his recording and publishing contract, but they have failed to deliver. The publisher doesn't want the artist to know that he's not in a recording obligation with them, because they are interested in eventually signing him to their record label of the same name.

You must understand that if you sign a publishing agreement, that you are not signed to a recording agreement. Understand that a publishers' role is different than of a record label. The artist didn't understand that his publisher couldn't stop him from creating opportunity and buzz for himself. He was expecting the publisher to promote him as an artist, but their job is only to promote him as a writer/composer. The artist is now upset with the publisher because he feels that the publisher isn't fulfilling his obligation. But when he signed the co-publishing agreement, he didn't understand that a publishers' role is not the same as a record label. As you can imagine, this is causing all sorts of conflict of interest and that's why you must fully understand contracts.

The artist took a $7,500 advance for 70% of his publishing share. Now the artist is about to hire a manager, who wants 20% of all income, including publishing. If he wants to secure a major record deal, I can only imagine the record label will want a percentage of his publishing as well. If he goes through and works with the new manager and a major record label he'll probably be left with 0% of his own publishing. This is really the worse case scenario and the artist has put himself in a really bad situation, from a music business standpoint.

After reading the artists recording deal, I then realized he was also in an ancillary rights deal (commonly referred to as a "360 deal") with the same producer that he gave 70% of his publishing and writer's share to. That means he's obligated to pay the producer another 20% of his gross income from any and all activities dealing with his career as an entertainer. The "360" is an exclusive recording contract between a record company and an artist in which, in addition to monies from sales of the artist's recorded music, the label shares in other income streams such as touring and live performance, merchandise, endorsements, appearances in movies and TV, and if the artist also writes songs, they also get a share of the publishing. So this means this artist actually signed a deal that allows the producer he signed with to take 90% of all of his revenue! He's so oblivious that he still seems interested in hiring this new manager, who wants another 20%, which would leave him at 110% owed. Therefore, he is working just to be in debt -10%. I'm so disgusted in this client after fully reading his contracts that I have no desire to work with him anymore. Under his current contracts, he'll barely have any money left to pay me for my time and consultation. Do not allow your ignorance of contracts, to allow you to give up 70% of your publishing rights and 20% of your gross revenue. This is called losing in the music business. The artist who signed this deal is a complete joke, in my opinion, and you'd be considered a joke too if you sign over 90% of your brand's income. The only scenario in which I could understand someone giving up 90% of their future revenue is if they were given a huge advance, in which he didn't receive. In fact, the advance that he received was already coming to him from the song that he made, that was placed on the Hollywood movie soundtrack. Had he just waited a few more months, he would have received over $7500 in music royalties from the work that he had already done, prior to signing the co-publishing deal, but he was too stupid and impatient to see that far ahead. If someone is willing to give you upfront money, always be leery.

The 360 deal is nothing new. The first reported 360 deal was English recording star Robbie Williams' deal with EMI in 2002. In the last few years 360 deals have become common place. New artists signing with a major label or their affiliates can expect it as a matter of course. The reason for the prevalence of the 360 deal is the dramatic decline in income from sales of recorded music. Income from sales of pre-recorded music reached its peak in 1999 at approximately 14.5 billion dollars. By 2012 that amount had shrunk to only approximately $7 billion - a decline of more than 50%, mainly due in part by the rise of the Internet.

Under the traditional paradigm, the label would pay the artist a small royalty, which was even smaller after all the deductions. The artist could expect to receive no recording royalty at all unless his album was a major commercial success. But he got to keep everything else: publishing, merchandise, touring, endorsements, etc. However, these days artists often generate more money from other activities than record sales. For instance, Lady Gaga's Monster Ball Tour grossed over $227 million dollars, and 50 Cent's deal with Vitamin Water turned golden when he accepted shares in the company in exchange for authorizing the use of his professional name in "Formula 50". It is reported that his shares were worth over $100 million after Coca-Cola purchased Vitamin Water's parent, Glacéau, for $4.1 billion. These developments have spurred the labels to seek to participate in all the possible revenue streams generated by an artist. I have seen small labels also known as production companies get in on the act and insist that new artists sign 360 deals with them even if they put little or no money into recording and make no promises in regard to marketing or promotion. These companies expect the artist to provide fully mastered recordings for little or no money upfront, and they demand income from all sources of revenue. Bottom line, these are horrible deals, if you are not getting the lion's share.

Record labels argue (and majors who pay big advances have more credibility in making these arguments) that they make significant investments in an artist's career by, among other things, putting up considerable sums for recording including paying advances to A-level producers, getting the artist's music on commercial radio, securing invitations for the artists to perform on popular television shows, paying for one or more top quality videos for YouTube and other outlets, and providing tour support before the artist is popular enough to demand significant sums for live performances. For emerging artists, a major label deal may be the path to becoming famous and rich. For instance, Lady Gaga was an unknown artist before Interscope spent a vast sum putting her on tour as an opening act for the New Kids on the Block, paying for marketing, hiring wardrobe and makeup, and paying all her other expenses for over a year, not to mention using their clout to get her invited as a guest on almost every important radio station in the country. The labels argue that 360 deals are fair because monies generated from touring, merchandise, endorsements, and other streams would not exist at all without their efforts.

Another topic I'd like to discuss is negotiating contracts. If you can learn to read contracts and understand the language in a contract, the next step to winning is negotiating your contracts. Most people are quick to sign the first thing someone presents them. What people fail to realize is that any contract can be altered. When someone gives you a contract, you are not obligated to agree to the terms. If you want, you can even have your own contract. Please remember that all contracts can be edited, by you. Remember that contracts are a mutual agreement. If you are unsatisfied with your contract, in any way, you can edit the contract to suit your wants and needs. You must come to a mutual agreement with the other party in which you are signing the contract with, before signing. Otherwise, you may find yourself regretting signing the contract, which can lead to resentment in your business relationship. If the contract deals with money, don't be scared to ask for more money. If the contract deals with a time period, don't be scared to shorten or lengthen it. Signing a contract means you agreed to the terms. Don't agree to anything that you will regret. Keep this in mind, before signing any contract you may encounter.

7 ALWAYS MAKE SURE YOU GET PAID FIRST!

With the exception that you are an artist, expect to get paid after your manager or label gets their share. If you are the manager, always make sure you get paid first. This rule is very important! Always put yourself at the highest point of the pyramid. Everyone eats, after you eat. Always structure your agreements so that the money comes thru you first. That's what being a boss really means. You delegate all funds. If you aren't dealing the money, then someone else will be... and your destiny will lie in their hands. People tend to forget about mutual agreements, when money is in their hands and they have control to delegate where funds go. Most people NEVER want to split up the pie. There are a few good people in the world who understand their roles and split up money fairly. Other than those select few, most people want 100% of everything. Never put yourself in the position where you have to ask for your own money. When the money doesn't come to you first, you put yourself in a very vulnerable position. I would hope that, when the money does come to you first, you do the right thing for your partners and split the money up accordingly, while being transparent as possible.

As a manager, you are responsible for the money. It's up to you to make sure the money gets in your hands first, so that it can be dispersed properly. Do not make the mistake of sending money, anywhere else, but to your address or bank account. The house always gets paid first. People will sign an agreement with you, but when the money comes, they tend to forget what they signed and catch faux amnesia. Save yourself the trouble and never put yourself in the position, where you have to ask for your own money. There are several great money transfer services now such as Cash App, PayPal, Venmo, and QuickPay that allow people to transfer money instantly. I mentioned those services because you may need to use one, to transfer money to your clients at some point.

You should never be in the position where you have to remind someone to give you your cut. Get your cut off the top. I hate to say it, but from my experience, when it comes to money, most people are really shady, especially if they're not used to having money. People's true colors tend to come out when a check arrives. Don't allow money to cause you and your clients to fall out in dispute. Money is a tool that you should be using to further your career. Money should not be a tool that causes conflict. More often than not, money is usually the number one reason for disputes.

I recently closed a sponsorship deal for a client (whom I don't work with anymore), with one of the biggest companies in the world. I made the mistake of not signing a management agreement with this client because he happens to be a family member. I was more interested in helping this family member, more than I was interested in capitalizing off of him. This was a mistake on my part. Upon his overnight success, I spent the next months setting up his online presence (using the skills I learned from Chapter 2), shooting original content for him, uploading videos and news clips that he was featured in, to the various accounts I set up for him, such as YouTube, Facebook, Twitter. I really was not interested in charging him any upfront fees for my management services. I've always had a passion for the type of work that I do and I really wanted to see him succeed. I figured that if I could close some sponsorship deals for him, then I'd eventually recoup my time investment, through the sponsorships that I helped to acquire. The original content that I created for him, led to a PR agent from the major company, reaching out to us. I negotiated a deal with the PR firm to shoot ten 1-5 minute web episodes for $5000. Although $5000 isn't much money, I knew that if we completed the first 10 episodes, it would open the door for more sponsorship opportunities. Companies love sponsoring clean brands that are self sufficient in creating content, especially if you have a large enough following online. The company that sponsored the content is a multi-billion dollar company, which spends tens of millions every year for advertising, promotion and sponsorship. I knew for a fact that the company would eventually have no problem cutting us a six-figure sponsorship check, if we could show them that we could get the ten episodes done for $5000. Major companies have no problem sponsoring social media influencers that create original content, which promote their products and brands. Companies want to align their products with content creators who have influence over their organic audiences.

After negotiating the deal, we signed a contract to produce the content and we planned to start shooting the content as soon as possible. The agreement stated that we would get paid the first half of the money, when we delivered the first 5 episodes. The remaining money would be paid as soon as the 10th episode was complete. I shot the first two episodes and the reps from the PR firm loved it. They were really excited to work with us and see the remaining 8 episodes. I underestimated the production costs and soon realized that it would be hard for us to complete the next few episodes, without the first half of the $5000. I told the reps that we needed them to send us a $2500 check towards the $5000, so that we could move forward with the production. The reps agreed and mailed the check for $2500.

I set up an LLC for the client, so that we could cash the check from the sponsorship deal. Prior to this deal, I only asked the client for 20%

commission on all deals that I closed, but this was a different situation. I actually had to close the deal and produce the content myself. Quality video productions take experience as well as time and money. I just so happen to be a jack-of-all-trades, and we didn't need to pay a production company, because I am a one-man production company. My client obviously didn't realize that I've spent the better half of my life, learning and becoming a master at producing Internet content. I make the production process look so effortless, that someone who doesn't know any better may think, they can do, what I do, on their own, which was a false pretense on his part. Like I said, I've been polishing my production skills, non-stop for the last 20 years. I could have easily told the PR reps to send the $2500 check to my address. I had the LLC articles of incorporation and the EIN number for the business already, so I could have went in the bank and opened a business account to cash the check. My plan was to split the check 50/50. I figured 20% for closing the deal and another 30% for my production costs, which was fair. Being my own production company, I have the freedom to charge what I want. I could have easily took the whole $2500 and not split it down the middle. I try my best to be fair and just. I was not interested in receiving the check. I have seen entertainment checks much bigger than $2500, so it wasn't a big deal to me. This being the biggest deal that I closed for him to date, I wanted him to get the check. I wanted him to see that my work was creating financial results. I really wanted it to sink in his head, that due to my hard work, checks were starting to come to his mailbox. This was a mistake on my part. The day before the check arrived, we spoke on the phone and I told him that I'd need 50% of the check, due to me being the one shooting, editing and producing the content, on top of being the manager and deal maker of the situation. He complied on the phone. The next day, I seen him emailing the PR reps saying, "I can't cash this check because it says LLC at the end of it, can you please reissue the check?". I was puzzled because up until this moment, I had been dealing with all of the correspondence with the PR firm. I immediately emailed the PR reps and told them that it was a misunderstanding and that everything was fine. Already embarrassed, I texted him and told him that we had an LLC already and that all he would need to do was open an account with the check and the LLC documents. Another day went by and I checked my account for the $1250, but my half of the check still wasn't there. Another day went by, and I noticed a deposit of $500 in my account. As I sat there puzzled, wondering why I was short $750, I soon realized $500 is 20% of $2500. That's when I realized that he wasn't a man of his word. He paid me based on management commission but he did not pay me for my production expenses. I depended on him to split the money up evenly, so that I could continue finishing the sponsorship deal. At this point, I demanded my $750. I spoke to him on the phone and he told me he spent my $750 already! I was shocked and I didn't expect this behavior from him, being a family member. Having respect for him, I didn't curse at him or say anything disrespectful. I got off the phone and called my father, who happens to be a very level headed intellectual.

When I spoke to my father about the situation, he suggested that I invoice the client for all the work that I had done, up to that point. I had never planned on invoicing him for what was almost 12 months of management work. When I calculated all of my expenses that I incurred while working on his behalf as his manager, it totaled over $7500 in management work and production, and I was being modest with my prices. I then emailed the client the invoice and explained to him my perspective of the situation in writing, being very careful of my words and explaining my situation to him, with all due respect. Within a few minutes of receiving the invoice and email, he called my phone speaking erratically, while cursing me out. He told me that he felt that he could find someone else to produce the content cheaper, and that I was out of line for sending him an invoice for $7500. He was very upset and I tried to reason with him, but he didn't want to hear my side, at all.

He then told me that he would deliver the remaining $750, when he could, and expressed that he had no plans to pay me my remaining $6250. He then changed the email address password that I created for him, which blocked me from further communicating with the PR reps. I was beyond shocked. More so disgusted than shocked. After working on his project for over a year, and closing a major sponsorship deal for him, this man had the audacity to spend my money, and then curse me out when I sent him an invoice, clearly showing the costs of all the production and management work I had already done for him. What an ungrateful piece of shit, I thought to myself.

Had I made sure I had gotten paid first, this would have never happened.

Now, that family member and me have not spoke, since the incident. All I can do is wonder and imagine what happened with the sponsorship deal. My plan was to finish the 8 episodes, then split the $5000, getting $2500 each. When it was time for the company to renew the sponsorship, I was planning to request $10,000 or more on the second round. Had we split the $10,000 evenly, I would have recouped the $7500 in time and expenses that I incurred while working on his project for the past 12 months. It never reached that point because I didn't make sure that I got paid FIRST! Don't let this happen to you. Get your money first. Most people, who are new to the entertainment business, really don't know how things work. As a creative, we often get underpaid and underestimated. People have even insulted me by saying things like, "you just sit around and press buttons all day", referring to me sitting at my laptop working. In my opinion, mental work can be just as stressful to the mind and body, as physical work. Don't allow anyone to underestimate your worth and undermine your value.

I have been sitting back waiting to see if he would be able to produce the remaining 8 episodes on his own, but so far, he hasn't been able to deliver. He doesn't know how to produce content and I believe he ruined the deal that I had in place with this major company, which is a big disappointment. Big brands pay millions of dollars for endorsement deals. I was sure that I could have gotten him a huge endorsement deal, but we never made it that far because I made the mistake of not paying myself first. In hindsight, I'm glad I was able to spot his shady ways, before any bigger deals took place. Don't let this happen to you. I later asked a friend of mine who is a Hollywood film and television commercial director, how much he would charge to shoot ten 1-5 minute web episodes. He told me his company charges $150k-225k per day. Don't let friends or family, undervalue your work and always make sure you get paid first. I'm still struggling with the mental pain and anguish from this situation to this day and it's made me very bitter and reluctant to work with friends and family. It's very unfortunate but from my experience, friends and family will usually be the first people to take advantage of you. Don't let a situation like this happen to you.

8 ONLINE MARKETING, ADVERTISING AND GOING VIRAL!

Next step is marketing your project. Now it's time to start using your website, blog, and all the social media platforms to promote your project. There is no definite right or wrong way to market your brand. The goal is to get your brand in front of people's faces. Do whatever works for you, to market your brand. I'd suggest keeping it classy and not spamming people, but that's just my opinion. Do whatever it takes to get your brand out there. The key to going viral is to cause people to have some sort of reaction. Your job is to make provocative content. People should feel some sort of emotion after digesting your content. If people don't feel any emotion after watching your advertisement or music video, then you're wasting your time and you should work on another campaign that does cause emotions to stir. Any emotion that your promotion causes is enough to help propel your project. Your job is to make people feel emotional. Whether it's love, hate, disgust, fear, anger, jealously, happiness, crying, smiling or laughter… any emotional reaction can lead to your video going viral. You are also trying to make people share your video, without the need to tell them to. You will never need to tell people to share your video, if you are already causing emotional reactions through your content. If people watch your content and it doesn't cause them to want to share it, then you will need to try again.

Viral Marketing is all about being indirect. If you tell someone what to do, you must consider that they may not do it. Sometimes you have to trick viewers into doing what you want them to do. Stop thinking about how you feel about your product and start thinking about how the viewer will react to your product. Also, if you cannot disconnect yourself from your ego, then you may never be able to create a viral video. What I mean by that is, don't get too caught up in any one campaign. If the campaign isn't working then you may need to try something else. Don't allow your ego to tell you that your campaign is good, when in fact, it's not yielding you any results. Be prepared to create a lot of content and do as many experiments as possible. Think of yourself as a scientist, trying to create the perfect potion. You only win through trial and error. Study other successful viral videos and study the emotional elements in the video, which you think may have caused the video to propel. There was a girl named Rebecca Black who had made a hit song that went viral in 2011 called "Friday". If you watch Rebecca's music video for "Friday" on YouTube, which now has over 110 million views, you will notice the dislikes on the video far outweigh the amount of likes on the video. The first time I watched the video and heard the song, I could understand why the video was starting to go viral. People hated her video so much, that they shared it with their friends. Doesn't that sound backward? People tend to spread their hate and that is why Rebecca's video went viral. Her video was very unconsciously corny, and it seemed unintentional. Rebecca Black now has over one million subscribers on YouTube and has made a career as a YouTube personality, because she made a video that most people thought was corny. Dislike is a conscious thought and emotion, and people love to share their thoughts and emotions on social media. Rebecca was rewarded with a viral video, thanks to people's hate for her music. It sounds backwards but that is exactly how viral marketing works. When possible, do your best to use reverse psychology, to deliver your messages. If you can cause people to react, then you have a hit, whether they love it or hate it. Hate and love are two of the strongest emotions. People love to share their hate online. You must also be careful when marketing, because if you go about your marketing wrong, you can easily cause people to hate you. If people truly hate you, they will not want to buy into anything you are selling. They may just come to your video to spew their hate and you may get plenty of views, but not plenty of sales. If you are in this business to make a living, then money should supersede the want for attention. You must find the balance. For your own sake, you must use your best judgment at times and I'd hope that in the process of marketing yourself, that you don't ruin your reputation. You must figure out a way to touch on people's emotions. While doing this, I suggested keeping your marketing classy. It's very easy to make classless videos that will turn people off. Be careful not to reveal your intentions or people will be turned off and they won't spread your videos as much. Your approach must seem real, natural and seem almost unintentional. There are a bunch of music artists who have viral videos, yet they never have real music careers, where they actually win awards, get radio play and make songs that actually chart. You must be careful when playing with people's emotions. The goal is to make people love you. If you can find people who love what you do, then they will buy whatever you are trying to sell. If you are planning to create negative emotions thru your marketing, make sure you are not the one in the video or advertisement, who is causing the negative emotion. Use actors or props, but never be the target in the video or ad, in which people hate. You may go viral but it won't help you to personally make money, with a negative image hanging over your head. People may hate you forever for a feeling that you projected in one video. That is why when a celebrity says something insensitive, any sponsors or endorsement deals may come to an end. In 2014, a recording of former Los Angeles Clippers owner Donald Sterling making racist remarks surfaced. Due to that recording, Sterling was banned from the NBA for life and was fined $2.5 million dollars. You don't want to say anything that may be racially insensitive or target any particular groups of people either. There's nothing wrong with using race relations while making controversial videos, but don't be insensitive while attempting to go viral. You can really ruin your brand, for life, if you go about your viral marketing wrong. Brands do not want to be associated with negative emotions. You must be very careful to cause the right emotions without it compromising yourself or your brand. There's a saying, any promotion is good promotion, but I can't totally agree with that. Keep in mind that marketing is very easy, when you actually have a good product that people want. It will be harder to sell a product that no one truly has a desire for. Spend most of your time, creating quality products to market. Have a purpose and give people a reason, to want to follow what you are doing or selling. Presentation is also key. Having a good graphic designer, who knows how to create great artwork, and having videographers and editors who can make compelling content, will help a lot with your marketing campaigns. When I was marketing my first DVD, which was a compilation of my short comedy movies, I used public access to market my brand. My show would come on locally twice a week. I would press up my own DVDs using my MacBook Pro, inkjet printable DVDs, and DVD cases and shrink wrap that I would buy from China Town in Manhattan. We would then go to Canal Street or Times Square to sell the DVDs one by one, on the streets. Often, no one knew who we were, and we'd have to pitch the product and sell ourselves, to make a sale. Other times, we'd bump into people that recognized us from the public access show. The fans of the public access show were always quick to buy and support our DVDs and merchandise. Nowadays, you can do effective marketing with no money, online. Using YouTube, Facebook, Twitter, Instagram and any other social media platform, you can really get your brand in front of people's faces, with minimal effort. Again, you will need the skills that I mentioned in Chapter 2, to effectively produce visual content, in which you can market online. Television advertising isn't expensive as you may think also. Every local cable TV network, allow regular people to purchase what is called "spot advertising". Spot advertising can be as cheap as $2-5 per commercial, depending on the network you'd like to advertise on, the time of day, and the length of your advertisement. Do as much research on spot advertising as you can. I won't go too much into spot advertising, because I have never used it to much success. I did run some spot advertising campaigns for a website that I own. I think Internet advertising is more cost efficient for an independent, and a lot more effective. When you advertise on television, it is harder to track your results. When you spend money on Internet advertising campaigns, you will be able to see exactly where your money went. Google AdWords, YouTube Video Ads, Facebook Ads, Twitter & Instagram are some examples of online advertising networks in which you can pay for promotion. With each of these networks, you can track your results in real time. These networks allow you to see how many impressions your advertisement received, how many people clicked on your advertisement, how many impressions your advertisement made (how many people possibly seen your ad), demographic data and geographical data. All of this information is very important and it will help you save money on your future campaigns. This data helps because it allows you to see exactly where and who your traffic is coming from, allowing you to fine tune your ad campaigns. Online advertising networks also allow you to target whichever city, state or country that you choose. If you are interested in doing television spot advertising, you will need to find out the local cable and television networks in the area you plan to target. You will then need to contact the spot advertising rep at the local network. They will then send you their rates and schedule. If you are interested in doing a national television advertising campaign (which can be very expensive), then there are companies that specialize in national spot advertising. Be ready to spend anywhere from $25k-$50k, for an effective national spot advertising campaign. Again, I've never used spot advertising to much success but have read plenty of stories about successful spot advertising campaigns. Joe Francis's "Girls Gone Wild" video series is a perfect example of a successful spot advertising story. At the time, "Girls Gone Wild" main form of marketing was late night television spot commercials. Times have changed since then, yet spot advertising can still be very effective, if you have the budget to do so. Some products work really well using spot advertisement such as the George Foreman Grill. I rarely see labels using television advertisements to promote music, unless it's a very successful musician. Television advertisement isn't the ideal way to market music nowadays, especially for an indie startup label.   I don't really recommend paying for advertisement early on, while building a music brand. I think building an organic fan base is the best way to go. It's pretty hard to sell people on music, with a commercial. People don't like to be force-fed. People like to discover music indirectly. Also, when you have to pay to play, then your music probably isn't that good. Word of mouth is the best form of advertisement, in my opinion. Marketing music on social media is probably the best form of advertising for music. Social media is based on word of mouth. Most people are followers and they tend to like, what everyone else likes. So if you can get past the initial stages of building an organic fan base, your music will continue to spread. How do you build an organic fan base? Again, there is no right or wrong way and everyone goes about it differently. I was able to build an organic fan base for my artist "iLoveMakonnen", that I signed in November 2011 through a website that I started in October 2009 called ILP. I started the ILP Video Network after my movie Criminals Gone Wild was ripped off by a website that I wont mention the name of. My movie was being illegally streamed for free, by this website while I was doing my television promotion for my film. I had an e-commerce website set up for CGW DVD sales, meanwhile, when someone would search the Internet for my film, this other website would show up above my own website, showcasing my film for free. I was pretty upset about this, and I did everything I could to stop my film from being illegally streamed. By the time the website removed my film, the actors in the movie folded and it was revealed that my movie, which I marketed as real, was really a hoax. I can only imagine how much money I actually lost, while that website was broadcasting my film for free. The owner of that website passed away at a young age recently. I wonder if his bad karma for ripping people off all these years finally caught up with him. Although we battled in business, finding out someone died is never good news and I wish nothing but the best for his family. I was so focused on not getting ripped off again, that I stopped producing content and spent the next few years of my life, building up the ILP Video website platform. One lesson I did learn from the website that ripped me off, is the exact reason why Walmart has dominated brick and mortar retail sales. The outlet that supplies everything, will beat the outlet that only sells one or a few products, EVERY TIME. Walmart is putting Toys R Us and many other "mom and pop stores" out of business, because Walmart not only sells toys, but they also sell groceries, electronics, home and garden equipment, sporting goods and almost anything else that you can think of. With the help of a web developer that I found in South America, we developed the ILP website and launched it in October 2009. I paid the website developer, using the money that we made from our Tunecore music sales. My brother AliAta and I would wake up everyday and post fresh new content on the ILP website. I would also rip my favorite HBO shows and clips from recent award shows, and other popular events, and repost the content on the ILP website. This was before Instagram and Facebook really blew up, and there were few streaming video media outlets. We would also post independent artists' music videos and promo clips, free of charge, while the website who ripped me off, were charging artists upwards of $500-750, for a single post on their website. I marketed ILP as the alternative to the rip-off website, and we started to grow really fast. By 2011, ILP was receiving upwards of half a million or more page views daily. ILP was also responsible for breaking some of the most popular hip hop acts to this day, yet we never truly received credit for the free promotion that we were giving to these independent artists. The website that ripped CGW off would usually contact the artists that we had our eyes set on, then post their content as if they were working in the artist interests, but it was really just to spite us. Being the bigger site, the artists that we promoted for free, would usually favor the bigger site that continued to rip us off daily, due to their larger audience. It was a very discouraging and we could never grow bigger than the rip-off website, because anything that we would discover and post on our website, they would just plagiarize it from us and claim it as their own content. They would get all the credit, and it started to feel like we were their employees, yet, we weren't getting paid to work for them. It was very discouraging. My brother and I were starting to generate income from ILP, yet we always had high monthly server bills due to our growing traffic and bandwidth usage. I can honestly say that ILP was one of the first websites to ever promote rapper "Future". We were promoting Future early in his career around the time when he released his "Dirty Sprite" mixtape. At the time, no other popular website that I knew of, was supporting Future's music. My brother introduced me to Future's music and I thought he was really talented. We continued to promote Future, until he caught the eye of popular rapper Drake. Future had a music video for his song "Tony Montana". We were the first website to post that video. A few months later, Drake made a remix to Future's "Tony Montana" and Future's career took off, landing him a major record deal with Epic Records. I was happy that Future's career was taking off. I really liked his music at the time and thought that he was a very talented artist. Future would later make a hit song with producer Sonny Digital, called "Racks On Racks" and his career continued to flourish. Little did I know, I would also later make a hit song with producer Sonny Digital. There were several other artists who I noticed were capitalizing off of the ILP traffic. Popular Internet rapper Lil B emailed ILP before he launched his solo career and we supported him heavily due in part to him already having a following in the Bay Area of California. ILP promoting Lil B, placed him in the middle of the war between ILP and the rip-off site. We would post one Lil B video then the rip-off site would post two of his videos. The next day, if Lil B would release three videos and we'd post them all, the next day the rip-off site would post four of his videos. It became a tit for tat situation where the rip-off site wanted to make it seem like they were responsible for the success of the artists that we promoted. The rip-off site knew we were on to something and they knew we were the creators of CGW, which had already gone viral. The rip-off site knew that we had a better eye for talent and viral content. His job was to make it seem like our eye for talent was really his eye. If people ever realized where the real source of his content was, then he probably would have gone out of business. The war between ILP and the rip-off site became very petty and it helped artists like Lil B gain millions of views and fans, free of charge, due to the traffic that ILP and the rip-off site were sending his way. We were providing the Internet with all of this daily content, yet we were constantly getting plagiarized and not truly capitalizing off of our work. That is when it dawned on me, that I needed to start signing artists. I couldn't allow another artist to become famous due to the ILP promotion, without us getting credit and a cut of the revenue. It just wasn't fair that we were working hard and helping artist to make millions, while not getting a share. I also knew that rip-off site would eventually start promoting any artists that we had signed, oblivious that they were actually working for us. I signed a rap group consisting of two friends, named Jonny Bravo & Swag Jesus. Previous to signing them, I would always post their content on ILP. I really enjoyed their music and videos, which always made me smile. I liked their music and thought they were very unique and quirky. I express mailed them both management agreements and they sent the agreements back soon after. On November 17, 2011, I got an email from someone named Makonnen Sheran. He was a fan of ILP and he wanted his video "Remix Me" posted on my website. I checked out his video and I thought it was different. I looked on his YouTube channel and listened to more of his music. I thought it was very unique so I emailed him and asked if he had a manager. He didn't have a manager and I soon sent him a management agreement also. He signed it and sent it back to me and I started working on building his brand online. At the time, he only had a YouTube channel with a couple music videos that he produced and a Soundcloud page with a few songs on it. On a random day, in 2012, while searching for fresh new videos to post on ILP, I came across a music video called "Bando" by a group named "The Migos". I really liked the song and posted it at the top of the ILP website in our featured video slot, just as we did with Future's and Lil B's videos. Soon after that, The Migos started blowing up. Rapper Gucci Mane signed Migos to a deal and their careers started to flourish. Soon after, they made a song called "Versace" which was very catchy. Soon after that, rapper Drake made a remix to their "Versace" song. I started wondering to myself, if this was a coincidence. Two artists that premiered on ILP, had gotten their songs remixed, by Drake, who is one of the most popular artists in the world, currently. Well-known rapper Lil Wayne (who Drake is signed to) also ended up making songs with Lil B around this time. To make a long story short, after working with Makonnen for 3 years, and promoting him nonstop on the ILP website, constantly, and creating hundreds of visuals with his music. Drake made a remix to his song "Tuesday", that we recorded at Metro Boomin's apartment with the production help of Sonny Digital. This confirmed that artists' were being broken through ILP, and it no longer seemed like a coincidence to me. My online outlet was working and it was responsible for the marketing, advertising, promotion and success of the iLoveMakonnen brand. After we got nominated for a Grammy Award for "Tuesday", producer Sonny Digital did an interview on NYC's Hot97 radio station where he credited ILP as the outlet that he discovered Makonnen's music, which led to our 2014 collaboration on the platinum selling "Tuesday" song. Creating an organic online network to promote your brand is key. It would have been impossible for me to grow ILP, had I only posted the content that I created myself. You cannot create enough content to keep up with the daily demand of viewers. It's best to create an outlet, which displays the best of everything, on the Internet. Nowadays, there are several social networking apps and websites, in which you can build your own online network of followers, without the need of maintaining a website with costly server bills and maintenance. I have also used "Facebook Groups", "Facebook Business Pages" and "Facebook Fan Pages" to some success. You can make a Facebook Group about any popular topic and people will naturally find your Facebook Group due to the millions of people who use Facebook's search feature daily. If you constantly add content to your Facebook Group or Facebook Fan Page, there's a possibly of growing a huge following, in the millions, which you can then use to promote your self-produced content as well. I recently made a Facebook Group about the Cleveland Cavs NBA Basketball team because a band that I manage, named "Red Rose Panic", made a theme song about the Cavs. I posted a bunch of recent photos and videos and links to current news stories relating to the Cavs and the NBA and within a few days this new Facebook Fan page that I created had over one thousand followers. By building a Facebook Group about the Cavs, my target audience, which was Cavs fans, was available to me when it was time to release the Cavs Theme Song. This is how you can use the Internet to find targeted niche audiences, without the need to spend money on ad campaigns. Use free social media websites to build organic outlets to promote your music brand. This same method works for outlets like Tumblr, YouTube, Twitter, Pinterest, Instagram and any other similar social media network app or website. Find out what your audience's interests are and build a community around that topic. When it's time to release your own promotion, your target audience will be at full attention. Rapper French Montana did the same thing to build his music career. I met French one day in 2005 on Canal Street while selling my comedy DVDs hand-to-hand in the streets of New York City. I was walking on Canal Street towards the Manhattan Bridge and me and French crossed paths. Judging by his age, he looked like my target audience. I decided to pitch French my DVD, with hopes that he would purchase it. After speaking with him he told me that he was also a DVD creator and asked me how much I was paying to manufacture my DVDs. French told me that he could beat whatever rates that I was paying for DVD manufacturing and also told me that he was the creator of the popular "Cocaine City" DVD series. At the time, Cocaine City was everywhere. There wasn't a store, that sold hip-hop mixtapes, that didn't sell French's DVD. Cocaine City DVD became popular because French learned to be a jack-of-all-trades (refer to Chapter 2). French would then interview the most popular rappers and shoot impromptu music videos for them. After getting the footage of the popular rappers for his DVD, he would then mix his music videos and brand in between the footage of the popular rappers. His DVD and affiliation with other popular artists in his DVD, helped him grow his "French Montana" and "Coke Boyz" brand. French soon started to become respected as one of the hottest underground rappers in New York and he soon landed a major recording deal with Sean "Diddy" Combs label Bad Boy Records. French's career has skyrocketed since then, he's sold millions of records and he has done a great job maintaining his relevance as a rapper and entertainer. I could never get my comedy DVD in stores, because the DVD sellers only wanted to buy DVDs that they knew they could sell. Not having any popular celebrity featured in my DVD, made it hard for me to get distribution. I had to come up with a product that was easier to market. A little over a year later, I came up wit the idea to make "Criminals Gone Wild". My goal at that time was to sell DVDs. This was before Internet streaming video really blew up and there was still a lot of money in physical DVD sales. I knew sex and violence sold and I knew that if I could make a film that showed realistic looking violence and crime, it would be sensationalized. In early 2007, AliAta and I started the production of CGW. After I came back from Hartford, CT, the Criminals Gone Wild trailer was out and was gaining traction on YouTube. Websites posted the DVD trailer, we did a few hundred thousand views, but then nothing really happened after that. We needed to get CGW on the news somehow. At the time, there were a few controversial DVDs on the streets. One called "Bum Fights" and another called "Crackheads Gone Wild". Both of the directors of those movies had been featured on the news regarding their shocking films. I had to figure out a way to get my movie on the news. Things were going slow and I ended up in a small town in Maryland, staying at my childhood friend Jonathan's house, about a two-hour drive from New York City. I was 25 at the time and felt like my life was at a dead end. It was cool to catch up with Jonathan after all these years. We lost communication for about 9 years, and I was grateful that he allowed me to stay at his house while I got a chance to figure out what I was going to do with my life. Jonathan had really turned his life around and I was glad to see him doing well. I had a desire to succeed and I remember it was hard to sleep at night knowing that I had a hot product that was in need of a promotional boost. After staying at Jonathan's house for some weeks, a news worthy incident happened in New York City called the "The A-Train Beatdown Video". A group of lesbian girls attacked an innocent man riding the subway and taped the attack, using their cell phone cameras. At the time, cell phone cameras were a new technology and YouTube was only 2 years old. No one had ever seen anything like this before. It was one of the first Internet videos, where criminals actually taped their crime, then shared it online for amusement. The news had a field day with the story and police were trying to find out the identity of the girls, who attacked the innocent man on the train. New York Daily News ran a story about the heinous attack and asked for the public's help in identifying the female suspects. Cell phone footage was really grainy back then, and it was hard to identify the girls' faces. At the end of the article that New York Daily News posted, it said "If you know anyone who appears in this video, please email csiemaszko@nydailynews.com". This was my chance to get Criminals Gone Wild on the news. I emailed the writer, Corky Siemaszko and said, "I don't know who those girls are in that A-Train beat down video, but I was attacked and robbed one day while walking home. While I was being robbed, I noticed a camera man was taping the whole incident. Word later got back to me that there is a man selling a DVD on the streets called "Criminals Gone Wild" that features my robbery! Please help me catch the guy who is making the DVD! This is very embarrassing for me." At the end of the email, I gave Corky my brother AliAta's phone number and told him to "contact me" if he had any questions. I went to sleep and didn't think anything of it. The next morning, my brother called me saying someone from the Daily News called him, talking about the DVD. My brother didn't know what was going on but he knew enough to play along. Soon after my brother called, I got a call on the other line from a writer from NY Daily News. I was walking to my car, in a grocery store parking lot at the time NY Daily News called. I spoke on the phone about the DVD for about 10 minutes and the writer asked me to email him a picture of myself. I emailed him a picture of myself as soon as I got back to Jonathan's house. At the time, I didn't really realize what was about to happen next. Before then, I had never been in the news and would have been happy with the smallest write up in the newspaper. The next day, I got a call fro AliAta. He said, "You need to get back to Brooklyn as soon as possible! There's a bunch of news vans lined up outside of the house!" He also told me that Daily News posted a full-page article on Page 7 of the NY Daily News, with my picture, mentioning Criminals Gone Wild. I was dubbed "The Most Depraved Director In New York". I immediately left Maryland and headed back to Brooklyn. It was the hottest story in the news and soon became one of the hottest trending stories around the world. I did at least 10 interviews in the coming days, with all of the major news outlets. At the time, I didn't even know who Bill O'Reilly was, but I would be on his show the next day. I then met Geraldo while leaving the Fox News network and he told me that he wanted to do an exclusive interview with me. Criminals Gone Wild had taken off and my PayPal account was blowing up with sales. The funny thing was, I really hadn't even released the movie yet. At the time, I had only released a three-minute trailer. I made about $2000 in online DVD sales that day through my website, criminalsgonewilddvd.com. The demand was bigger than the supply and I had to quickly get thousands of DVDs made. Criminals Gone Wild became a viral success and to this day, the CGW videos on YouTube receive tens of thousands of views per month. The CGW videos also helped fuel the early traffic to the ILP website. I posted video clips on the CGW website which I then redirected to be viewed on the ILP website. It would have been harder for me to get ILP website off the ground, had I not had organic traffic flowing to ILP through the CGW website and YouTube content. You cannot plan for these types of events to happen. All you can do is be ready, when they do happen. Being ready means having a good product for sale, as soon as you create a big enough demand. Nowadays, people seem more concerned about generally being on social media websites, than actually having a product to offer the viewers on social media. You have to do something that catches people's attention, if you want to make sales. Just being on social media websites, isn't enough. Just making music and putting out videos, isn't enough. You need to find some type of edge that will make you stand out from today's oversaturated social media crowd. Controversy always works. Now, everyone has a camera phone. Everyone knows how to shoot video and everyone claims to be a director. It's even harder to break through now with the rise of fake news. I consider myself one of the pioneers of fake news and reality shows. Besides MTV's the Real World, there weren't many reality shows when Criminals Gone Wild came out. We were really ahead of our time. Criminals Gone Wild went viral before the term "viral video" became a household phrase. Marketing and going viral is about being ahead of the times. Finding a demand and being ahead of the curve. Study what has worked for other people. Study other people's success stories, and emulate. Had I not studied the success of "Girls Gone Wild", "Bum Fights", "Crackheads Gone Wild" & "Cocaine City", then I would have never had success with "Criminals Gone Wild". Another reason French Montana's Cocaine City DVD was a success was because the artwork. At the time, "Grand Theft Auto III" was one of the top selling videos games. French Montana's "Cocaine City" DVD cover artwork looked just like the cover of the GTA III video game cover. French emulated a successful video game franchise's art and soon his DVD started selling out too. Don't let your ego get in the way of copying the ideas of great minds. French found a product that was already a hot seller, and made his products artwork look the same. Some people will call it copying while some people may call it genius. Whatever the case may be, French made a lot of money from Cocaine City DVDs and those sales helped him to launch his highly successful music career. This is very similar to what we did with the Soulja Unit project. I like to study the iTunes and Spotify charts. It's a great barometer to see who and what songs are buzzing. When I'm studying the charts, I'm mainly looking for artists that I never heard of. I then check to see what record label that artist is on. It's rare to find an artist, who isn't on a major label, yet, still make it to the charts. If you can make it on the iTunes or Spotify charts, without the help of a label, then you are really doing something special and you are worth being studied. I then do research on the artist. I check their different social media pages and see what their following is like. I look at their videos, their website, and I try my best to pinpoint where they are getting enough traffic to translate into record sales or streams. Any successful artist that makes it to the iTunes or Spotify charts, with simple research, you can usually track their success, easily. I remember when I first heard about the group "LMFAO". With little research, I found out that they were the son and grandson of music legend Barry Gordy. No one makes it to the charts by accident. There is usually a source of buzz that can be traced. Do your research. Find out how they got there. In my opinion, paid advertising will not create create buzz for an indie music startup, unless you are spending hundreds of thousands or even millions. Buzz means that people are actually searching for you, without you needing to pay for them to look at you, which means people are truly interested in your campaign. People still search for Criminals Gone Wild to this day, and I've never paid a cent to advertise the movie. Paid advertisement compliments buzz. Paid advertising is like icing on the cake. Some products work very well with paid advertisement, such as a product like "Girls Gone Wild", which is sex-related. Straight men are naturally thinking about sex and hot women, so the paid Girl Gone Wild campaigns play off of something that men already desire. People don't necessarily desire music. People desire money, sex, food, cars, nice clothing, and things of that nature. That is why paid advertisement can work in those scenarios. I believe music is different. Paid advertising, in music, works better for established artists, more so than unknown artists. If you're fortunate enough to have a lot of money to work on your music campaign, don't think that throwing a bunch of money at it, is going to get you buzzing.

Good music and good visuals, get artists buzzing. Nowadays, I notice that there are more artists who are famous for their antics on social media, more so than for their music. I can name a bunch of artists right now, that I know their name and face, but I haven't heard any decent music from them. I'm assuming these artists figure, if they can get a large following, then people will begin to like their music. This isn't necessarily true. There's a bunch of artists who are on TV reality shows, and have large followings on Instagram and other platforms, yet they still never make it to the music charts. The music business is about making music. Use social media to your advantage, but don't use it to make a clown out of yourself and your brand. If you are trying to make it in the music business, you probably don't want to be known as "the funny guy from Instagram". Making silly videos for people to laugh and you, has worked for a few artists, but I wouldn't recommend it. If you study some of the biggest artists, they tend to stay away from the social media antics. This is just my opinion, based off my own personal research. If you want to be an Instagram clown, then that's your prerogative. There is nothing wrong with being a clown, if that's what you decide to do with your life. There are plenty of professional clowns who make careers entertaining people. I'm just giving you my professional perspective on the topic of the music business and if you want people to take your music seriously, then I wouldn't suggest being an Internet comedian as a way of promoting your music. The Weeknd, another artist who has blown up due in part to the Internet and has become one of the biggest stars of the decade, always came across, serious. I've never seen any videos of The Weeknd, making a clown of himself. I rarely even see pictures of him smiling. Not to say that you can't smile. By all means be yourself. I just think that if you want people to take your music seriously, then you shouldn't come off as some sort of jester. There are some artists that I notice on the charts, who have huge followings on YouTube, and have built their channels around playing videos games, doing pranks videos or comedy videos. There's nothing wrong with that, but I have yet to see a YouTube prankster or comedian, really break through in the music business, besides having a song or two, that does a decent amount of downloads/streams. These "YouTubers" are people who have real fans who may support their music, but they rarely get support from DJs at the radio stations and nightclubs who could possible play their music and spread it to a larger audience. Music gatekeepers, like music writers, bloggers and DJs, who devote their lives to music, usually hate on Internet sensations that turn into musicians. Most DJs won't support these kinds of artists, unless they really have a strong single that breaks through, somehow. I don't know of any YouTube comedians or prankster that has dominated the music world, and has gone mainstream. There is a guy named KSI from the UK who has had some major success in the music business, due to his

YouTube gaming channel that currently has over 16 million subscribers. He is a rare case and I have honestly never heard any of his music, but I have seen his name on the iTunes charts a few times. There is also a rapper named Logic that I've heard is considered a "nerdcore" rapper, who has a YouTube gaming channel, but I remember hearing about him being a rapper, before I heard that he was a gamer. Another thing I want to discuss is the term "viral". The word is used very loosely nowadays and I don't think most people really know the true meaning of it. I was talking to this woman one day, and she was about to release her music video and she said to me, "we're wrapping up the editing and working on making the video more viral". I automatically realized that she didn't really know what she was talking about. You can't "make something more viral". You can make a video and plan for it to go viral, but the actual act of a video going viral and spreading to millions of people is somewhat of a natural phenomenon. I like to compare it to planting a seed in the ground. You can't make a tree. I can make a tree out of clay, but I can't make a real life natural tree. You can plant a seed, buy some good soil, and water a tree so that it grows, but you aren't really making a tree. The seed makes the tree. The sun makes the tree. The soil makes the tree. You can only plant the seed, but you didn't actually make the tree. The growth of a tree is a natural phenomenon that happens. Just like you can't make a human. You can have sex and inject sperm into a woman, but you aren't really "making a child". The birth of a child and the growth of a human, inside of a woman's womb, is something that is way beyond us as humans and it is the perfect example of a natural phenomenon. I personally cannot make a brain. The growth of a brain inside of a woman's uterus is beyond my power. Yes, the sperm may come from my body and my body may have made the sperm, but did I actually make a human brain? Debatable to say the least, but I hope you understand where I'm coming from. I believe a viral video is somewhat of a miracle and phenomenon. Causing millions of people to react emotionally in a short amount of time, while getting your message across is a truly amazing feat. I've seen large corporations such as Pepsi create viral video campaigns. These videos aren't real viral videos, in my opinion. These major corporations' "viral videos" go "viral" because they pay to make them go "viral". A true viral video happens organically and will do millions of views, without the need for the creator to spend millions on production and marketing. Of course if I make a commercial with LeBron James dressed up as an old man dunking on kids, while he's drinking a Sprite, millions of people will see it, because LeBron is already known by millions and so is Sprite. These manufactured "viral videos" are backed by the finances of major corporations. That is not my opinion of a true viral video. That's called a paid advertisement. Paying the NFL a million dollars to show your commercial during the Super Bowl, is not considered going viral.

Yes, a bunch of people may have seen your advertisement, but that's not what going viral means. Don't get the term confused. In most cases, going viral is not something you plan. Most true viral videos were not made with the intention of going viral. With all of this being said, study true viral videos and not the fake viral videos, which have been backed by major companies with million dollar budgets. Let's talk about SEO, which stands for Search Engine Optimization. I spent lots of years practicing different SEO techniques. What you are trying to achieve through SEO is better search engine ranking. Better search engine ranking means that your website, video or product, shows up on page one of search engine results page (SERP). If you can get your products listed in the first place on page one, then you will receive all the traffic, for that given search term, which could mean thousands or millions of organic hits, views, subscribers, sales, by the second. There are different SEO methods for different search engines and websites. For example, Google bases their results based on seniority, contextual content and a few other factors. Google usually post sites that have been around longer, on the first page. There used to be ways to manipulate Google's search engine listings, for shorter keywords, but they are constantly changing their algorithm and making it harder for people to market. Google would rather you spend money with their AdWords program, than you find a way to beat their system. There are still millions of keywords that you can do minimal SEO on, and still rank well. Don't get too caught up in SEO and don't let anyone convince you into paying for SEO, if you really can't afford it. When you pay for SEO, you also may not know whether the person you are paying is using Whitehat or Blackhat techniques. White Hat SEO is the opposite of Black Hat SEO. Generally, White Hat SEO refers to any practice that improves your search performance on a search engine results page while maintaining the integrity of your website and staying within the search engines' terms of service. My new Whitehat SEO methods don't consist of attempting to cheat the search engines. If you follow the rules, you will definitely see your posts, ranking well in the different search engines. Some websites such as Facebook, rank search data based on your following. For example, if I search for "Chicago Bulls" in Facebook, the page with the most followers or the post with the most shares will show up at the top of the search results. You won't get a lot of shares if you don't have a lot of followers, but if you can get a lot of shares on a post, it will help you to gain new followers. Find ways to get people to share your content, and that will help jumpstart anything that you post online. Instagram, Facebook and Twitter all seem to work this way. Google and YouTube are a little different. There was a time on YouTube where the videos and the search results were easy to manipulate. That has changed drastically in the past few years. There was a time where the related videos on YouTube, were strictly based on title and video tags. Now,

YouTube (Google) has their own algorithms where they try to decide what videos you want to see next instead of simply placing videos with related content. I don't know if it was a combination of them trying to stop people from manipulating the system, or whether it was to stop a bunch of spam content from showing up in the related video results, which would probably cause YouTube to lose traffic. YouTube totally switched everything up, so that you can't win unless you play by their rules. If you play by Google's (YouTube) rules, they will reward you with tons of traffic. But you must follow these steps.   Something I learned last week, YouTube doesn't like when you send people away from YouTube. While building your channel, when uploading videos, do not post links to your social media pages, drifting people away from YouTube. Posting links to other YouTube videos and playlists is fine but do not promote your website in the description of your video. If you must promote your other websites, make sure they aren't hyperlinks (remove the http:// from the link). Instead of sending people to your other social media pages, put a Subscribe link in your YouTube description. If you must promote outside links on your YouTube videos, use Google URL Shortner for your links. I still haven't had a chance to determine whether or not YouTube still penalizes you for sending people from YouTube, even when you use their short links or not, so I'd recommend finding other ways to promote your various websites and social media pages. You can always put links to your other websites in your video also.   Post content as often as possible. You really want to be posting new content, every day, if you want to build a following on YouTube, fast. Learn how to make attractive and easy to read thumbnails. This goes back to knowing how to use Adobe Photoshop. If you can't do it, have your designer make your YouTube thumbnails more attractive. Study other YouTube creators who have millions of subscribers and study how their video thumbnails look. Make your thumbnails look more like the thumbnails of YouTube users with millions of subscribers. The thumbnail is very important. You want to always have the most click worthy thumbnail as possible.   I recommend writing as much original content in the video description. Google loves contextual content. The more words you put in your description, the better. Talk about your video. Who shot it? Who produced it? Where were you at when you shot it? Write as much detailed and relatable information about the video as possible.   Study other channels with content similar to the content that you plan on posting. Go to their video listing page and scroll to the very bottom to see their first video. Study the progression. Study which of their videos, have done the most views. Emulate as much information from popular channels as possible. The formula to win is already laid out, whether you realize it or not. Study the winners and do what the winners are doing. Of course you don't have to do the exact same thing they are doing. I'm speaking of release frequency, production value, video topics. Study Google Trends, study the Trending Videos on YouTube and see what people are talking about that week. Make content with themes surrounded by what's going on in the news or in the world. That is how you will get tons of organic search engine traffic. People search for what's popular, at any given time. Be fast to churn out content also. The faster you can produce and release your content, surrounded by the most relevant topics, the more traffic that you will receive. Do your best to predict what will happen, and be ready to have content to release, upon your predictions coming into fruition. I'm speaking in general about how to build a YouTube channel, but sticking to the topic of music brand growth, study "Boyce Avenue" and their YouTube channel's progression. Every artist that I work with, I tell them to study "Boyce Avenue", but it usually goes in one ear and out the other. Over the years, I've watched Boyce Avenue grow their music YouTube channel to almost 10 million subscribers. I have followed Boyce Avenue since 2009 and it amazes me to see how far they've come. The success formula is right there for you to study. It's no mystery and it's not rocket science. Cover songs are the way to break through in the music business. You can remake any song by anybody and you can sell it, as long as you send the publisher a "compulsory license" of your intend to sell and pay the publishing royalty rate per sale. Boyce Avenue has built their following as a cover song band. They remake popular hit songs and reap all the benefits of the major label promotion, without being signed to a major record label. They are an indie band and they've released over 30 albums on online music stores, and have based their success around remaking popular songs. It seems to be working well for them. They have their own record label called 3 Peace Records where they release their cover albums on iTunes, Spotify, Amazon and all of the other digital music stores. If you do exactly what Boyce Avenue is doing, then you can't lose. There are plenty other singers on YouTube who have built their fan base around making cover songs. When I tell new artists to make cover songs, they often get offended as if I'm suggesting that they don't have enough talent to write their own original hit songs. The fact of the matter is, if you aren't popular already and you don't already have people following your music brand, then no one will be looking to hear your originally written songs. Your best bet is to swallow your pride and align yourself with other popular artists, by making cover songs, remixes and remakes. Like I said, you can also profit using a compulsory license as well, so there's also a financial incentive to making cover songs, yet most artist will never swallow their pride and sing other people's songs. I beg every artist I work with to make cover songs. They rarely listen to me. I told an artist this yesterday, "If Pharrell Williams wrote a song for you and gave it to you to perform, you'd perform it, right?". The artist answered, "Yes, of course, it's Pharrell." I then asked him, "Well then what's the difference in doing a Pharrell cover?". He was speechless. Don't let your pride and ego get in the way of doing what's practical to promote your brand. Making cover songs are in complete good taste and sometimes people may love your cover songs more than the original artist's version. Once you build a solid following by remaking popular songs, you can easily market your own, original music, to your new fans. It's never too late to release your original music. Realize and accept you're your brand isn't big enough yet and millions of people aren't searching for your original music, yet there are millions of people searching for Pharrell's music already. Align yourself with what's already working, if you want to succeed fast. There are some artists who released tons of original music and became successful, such as my former artist iLoveMakonnen, but that was a rare case on top of the fact that he had me, who happens to be an online marketing expert, working his project for three years. There is artist named Russ who I've been following for some time now, who released lots of music in the same fashion that I did with the iLoveMakonnen project, and he recently became a huge success and has gone multi-platinum. Again, do what works for you. I'm just attempting to give you ideas, so that you never reach a dead end, while trying to promote your music brand. When researching what cover songs to make, what you have to do is find a song that just came out or a song that has been out for a short time, that you believe will start picking up traction later and then make a remake of the song before everyone else does. After recording the cover song, make a quick music video of the cover song or remake, and post it on YouTube and other social media websites. If you properly title and tag your video, people will find your video because people are already searching for popular songs, which are being played on TV and radio, every few minutes. Once you accept the fact that no one is really looking for your music yet, you can commit to methods, which will help people, find your music. Some people will think you're just a copycat, and wonder why you get a kick out of singing other people's songs, but don't pay that any mind. What you are doing is using what's already popular, to your advantage. Why spent a million dollars on marketing if the major label already spent a million on marketing? Remember, there's nothing new under the sun anyway. I've even seen examples where people made covers of popular songs, and then the cover song became bigger than the original song. This has actually happened with my song "Tuesday". I co-wrote "Tuesday" back in 2014. The song was a hit in the USA, but it didn't do too well overseas. Fast-forward to 2016, a Turkish DJ named Burak Yeter, made a new cover version of "Tuesday" and released it. In 6 months, the new "Tuesday" song's music video had already surpassed the original "Tuesday" music video in views. I never imagined anything like this happening to one of my songs and it's been a great blessing. Before "Tuesday", Burak never had a hit that big. Now he is touring the world and getting international recognition off a song that he didn't even write. That's how the music business works. Cover songs are the way to go. If you want to build a large following on YouTube, Spotify, and other social media websites, I'd recommend remaking current songs, which are already popular. You can't lose if you do this. Back to SEO, after you're in the flow of releasing at least one new cover song every week, the next step is reposting your video on as many different pages as possible. What you are doing is attempting to create "backlinks". Backlinks have always been a staple in good SEO. Most SEO is based on the amount of backlinks you have. Every time your video is posted on a different website, it gives the video and the video link, more power. If you can get your video posted on at least 5 different websites, then your video may rank well on YouTube search results. I've noticed that at times, when you don't create backlinks for your videos, YouTube won't even show your video in their search engine results. Now it's time to use Blogger, Wordpress, Tumblr, Facebook, Twitter, Instagram. You want to repost the video on your Blogger site and your Wordpress site. Yes, have both. Make sure to embed the video and put the URL link, hyperlinked, under the video embed. That way there's a text link and an embed code. You may even want to hyperlink the title of the video, under the video player. The more sites you own, then the more backlinks you can create for your videos. Repost the video on Tumblr next. Repost the video on Facebook. Sign up to some Facebook groups with nice amounts of followers and repost your video link in there. Repost your video link on Twitter and add your latest video link in your Instagram profile. I also sign up to different music forums and start forum threads with the video link. 4chan is a good place to repost your video link. Reddit also. I also use a site called MyVidster. When you are posting on these forums, make sure your headlines are attractive. Make titles that would entice people to click on them. We call this "click bait". Click bait is only frowned upon when the content isn't good. I like click bait titles because they get my attention. I am only disappointing in the click bait titles when the content fails to deliver on the subject in which I was baited into clicking on. Use click bait to your advantage. The key is to post your content in as many places as possible and you will start showing up in the YouTube and Google search results, as well as the many other search engines. Also study how other popular high viewed videos on YouTube are titled. The way you title your video is very important. Make sure to use the same titling format, as the other popular videos, until you figure out what works best. Also, make sure you tag your videos properly on YouTube. I notice that most people don't know how to tag and they'll use a bunch of irrelevant words that nobody searches for in their tags. Only use high searched words that relate to your video in your tags. If you are unsure of what keywords are highly searched, then you will need to start studying

Google Keyword Planner. Log into Keyword Planner and compare different search phrases. Keyword planner allows you to see exactly how much traffic your keywords are getting every month. Only use high traffic keywords to tag your videos. Also, do your best to narrow your keywords down to niche keywords. Niche keywords may have less search volume, but there is less competition to rank high for those keywords. Also, sign up to Google Analytics and put trackers on all of your web properties. It's good to be able to see what's going on with your websites and study your traffic sources and demographic data. For every video you upload to YouTube, you need to create a one-minute version to upload on Instagram. Twitter also allows you to upload videos up to 2 minutes 20 seconds. If you don't know how to download videos from YouTube, to re-upload on Facebook (and vice-verse), you can use a site called KeepVid or DownVids. I like to use KeepVid and DownVids because when you upload a HD video to YouTube, it automatically gets converted to a lower file size, yet it remains in great quality. If your phone will not allow you to save big video files, you may need to convert smaller file size versions of your video, for Instagram uploading. Vimeo, DailyMotion, Break, AudioMack are also some other good video and audio social media sites that you should sign up to. Get accounts on YouTube, Twitter, Facebook, Vimeo, Soundcloud, AudioMack, Instagram, Google+, Tumblr, Blogger, Wordpress, at the very least. Sign up to as many sites and possible and always link back to all of your various social media accounts, on your profile. What you're doing is creating a web of links, that all come back to each other. Think of it like a spider web, the bigger your web, the more insects you will catch. WWW stands for World Wide Web. This is how you control the Internet, by making a big web that all links back to you. This is what Google and YouTube check for when they decide if your content will show up on the first page of their search results. For your brand, you must come up with a good name, and stick with it. Make sure your social media name is the same on ALL accounts. You don't want your Instagram account to be @Madonna but your Twitter is @Madonna_1458 and then your Soundcloud name is @MadonnaMusic. Find one name that no one else has claimed, and make all of your social media names the same. If your name is taken, then you will need to come up with another name or add something to the name to make it unique, like @TheOnlyMadonna or @MadonnaMusic or @iamMadonna or @TheRealMadonna. Continuity is very important. Don't have a bunch of different social media names. It makes your brand look silly and unprofessional. I hope I am not speaking too vaguely and I hope what I've written, makes sense to you. It is up to you to research these marketing methods on your own, while learning and coming to your own conclusions. These methods that I wrote are the exact methods I've used to generate hundreds of millions of views to various videos I've upload to YouTube. My ILP website has also received over half a billion page views of organic traffic, since I launched it in 2009. Another issue about marketing that I'd like to discuss is, how some people only market themselves on one platform. In my opinion, YouTube should be one of your main channels for marketing your content. Every other video site that you may upload content to, such as Vimeo or DailyMotion, should be a mirror of your YouTube channel content. I see way too many artists who solely focus on their Instagram page. There are some people who have built large audiences, solely from using one platform to market themselves. If the goal is to succeed in the music and entertainment business, then you need to be marketing yourself to as many audiences on as many platforms as possible. YouTube is the perfect platform to upload long-form content. If you are a musician, you need to be uploading new content every week, if not every day. If you don't have a music video to upload, then find something else, related to your music, to make a video about. Upload that content on the YouTube channel and then take a one-minute clip from that video, and promote it on Instagram and other mobile media platforms like Twitter. Uploading your content only on Instagram is a mistake because if Instagram gets shut down, then everything you worked for will disappear. You must use as many marketing channels as possible, to promote your brand. Remember, Instagram is only one place. A lot of artists nowadays seem to believe that Instagram is the only place to market. Instagram is just one avenue. Your work needs to be seen everywhere. People like Instagram because it doesn't take much thought. You can just pull your phone out your pocket, record a video, and then it's on the Internet. It's become a gift and a curse because I see people spending the majority of their day on Instagram, looking at what other people are doing and uploading videos to Instagram, but they are neglecting the other outlets in which they can be building their brand. Don't make this mistake. I recently purchased a Sony Bravia LCD Smart TV last year, which is a TV running on the Android operating system, which is what most smartphones use, with the exception of iPhones. If you already own a "smart televisions" then you'd know that most of them come with the YouTube app, pre-installed. YouTube is no longer some distant world, only accessible by geeks and nerds who spent all day on their computers. YouTube is now very mainstream and in the next few years, the majority of the televisions in the World will come equipped with the YouTube app pre-installed. People are also getting tired of expensive cable and satellite bills and are becoming "cord cutters". Cord cutters are people who solely use the Internet to get their daily visual and audio content and they don't bother paying landline phone bills, because they are using VoIP (voice-over-IP). They don't pay for cable TV bills because they download or stream all of their shows, using their Internet connection. Most major television networks have their own Android App that you can download and use to watch the shows you enjoy, without actually needing cable service. Recent statistics show that friends and family are the primary source of music discovery (22 percent), though radio still gives streaming a run for its money. Online, YouTube is the most popular platform for finding new music with 15 percent of people using it most often to stay up to date with music, in 2017. Spotify is the second most popular choice for online music explorers (10 percent) followed by Pandora (9 percent).

9 SPLIT SHEETS

Split sheets are used to determine how much each person involved with a song, contributed. If you made a song on your own, that being the music (or the beat/instrumental) and you wrote the lyrics, then you own 100% of the song and there is nothing to split up. But if you only wrote the lyrics to the song and a producer made the beat, then you and that producer need to sign a split sheet together stating that the two of you created the music and lyrics and that you are splitting the song 50/50. There are different ways that you can split up a song, depending on the amount of contribution that you made to the song. For example, one person may have come up with the hook to the song, one person may come up with the lyrics and another made the beat. There are a few ways you can split up the song. Typically, the producer of the music gets 50% of the song and the other 50% is split up between the writers. The two writers may agree that the hook is worth 20% and the verse is worth 30%. So the split sheet would say Producer 50%, Hook 20%, Verse 30%. Then all parties will list their name and which part they contributed and then all will need to agree and sign the split sheet, to make it official. The split sheet protects every one from future disputes about who contributed what and ensures that every party gets their fair share of the song royalties. In some cases, depending on the relationship of the parties involved in the song, the song may be split evenly. So three people would split the song up 33.33%, 33.33%, 33.34% to total 100%. Split sheets must always total 100%. I know a guy who wrote a dozens of hit songs, but he was oblivious as to what a split sheet was and how split sheets worked, at the time of writing the hit songs. This guy has literally helped to write various full albums that have gone multi-platinum and he's written countless hit songs over the years, for an artist that he was in a boyfriend/girlfriend relationship with. Yet, when I search his name on ASCAP or BMI's publishing info database, his name doesn't show up on

ANY of the songs that he was a part of! What that means is, he never signed any split sheets, therefore he gets NO credit on ANY of the songs as a songwriter/composer. When you get no credit and you're not on the split sheets, then you get NO royalties. You understand? You don't get ANY money. If you write a song, you automatically are entitled to a portion of the copyright and publishing. If you don't claim your share, then nobody will claim it for you, and they'll keep the points for themself. Why not? There is no sympathy for ignorance in the music business. Had I known him at the time all of this was happening, he'd be a rich man to this day. Literally, millions lost and no proof that he had any claim to the songs other than his word against the people who already collected and spent the his royalty money. Imagine losing a winning Mega Millions Lottery Ticket... yea, that's him. He's now attempting to sue for royalty money that was already spent and he has no real proof that he had anything to do with any of the songs that he claims he wrote. It's really a sad story and I feel horrible for him, but that's the way things go in the music business. If you don't educate yourself on how the business really works, then you will come out a loser. The real wealth that's made in the music business derives from split sheets and publishing royalties. We'll talk more about publishing royalties and setting up a publishing company in the next chapter

10 WHAT IS PUBLISHING?

There is actually 200% of a song. There is 100% of the writer/composer share and then there's 100% of the publishing share. Think of it as 2 pizza pies. Every time you make a song, you and whomever you created the song with, will be splitting up two pizzas. As songwriter/composer, you are automatically entitled to an equal share of both pizzas, depending on your contribution share of the song. You are automatically the publisher of your share of the song you wrote/composed, unless you designate your publishing rights to a third party publisher. You will need to set up an LLC to collect your publishing royalties and you will need to sign up to a PRO (Performing Rights Society) such as ASCAP or BMI. You may designate all or some of your publishing share to a third party publisher for several reasons. One reason being, you may want to work with that publisher, because they can help you further exploit the song, which could lead to more exposure of your song. Another reason is that the publisher can help get you sessions with other popular artists or producers, that they may work with, which may heighten your chances of making songs that will generate revenue. Another reason may be that the third party publisher is willing to give you an advance on your future publishing royalties. The advance amount may determine how much of your publishing share that you will be giving up. When a publisher gives you an advance, they are taking a risk. There is a possibility that the third party publisher may not recoup the advance that they have given you. Publishers take a risk when they give advances, so in return for that risk, you may be splitting your publishing share 50/50 with the publishing company, or the publishing company may give you a bigger advance, for a 25/75 split. It all depends on your publishing agreement, so read it carefully. Your advance amount may also depend on your track record as a producer or how big of a hit the song is, in which you are trying to get an advance against. Sometimes publishers will do one-off deals for a single or do long term publishing deals with a producer or writer who they believe will make lots of money over a period of time and have a long career. It all depends on the situation. Publishing companies are usually only interested in advancing money, if you have a hit song or a song that seems to be gaining momentum and/or is getting radio play. A song is only worth something a publisher when it becomes popular. Publishers aren't interested in songs that aren't popular yet unless you are someone like Jay Z or Garth Brooks, who has a proven track record of releasing hit songs. In that case, Jay Z may be able to get a multi-million dollar advance from his publishing company, before he even releases a new album, because the chances are very good that the publisher will recoup their money, knowing Jay Z's track record of selling over a million records per album. Building your catalog, reputation and creating hits is what determines how much money you will make from publishing and how much money a publishing company may offer to advance you. Another reason why people are against record deals is because record companies want a piece of your publishing. I've even heard stories about artists signing deals where they receive none of their publishing and gave up 100% of it to the label. That's the dumbest thing you can do, unless of course the label paid you up front for a lifetimes worth of publishing. But there's no real way to determine what a lifetimes worth of publishing is worth, because you never really know what's going to happen with a song. You don't know if they're going to use your music as the theme song of the Spiderman Movie that comes out in the year 2028. You didn't know Toyota was going to put your song in their commercial for the 2021 Camry campaign. You don't know what's going to happen in the future. That's why you want to retain as much of your publishing rights as possible. In 1981, Queen and David Bowie didn't know a rapper named Vanilla Ice would sample their song "Under Pressure" and make the hit song called "Ice Ice Baby" in 1990. You can't predict the future. Hold on to your publishing. You may be sitting on millions of dollars in the future while not even realizing it. Two years ago, I didn't know who Burak Yeter was. Today, I check for him because his new song that I wrote in 2014 is doing two million streams a day on YouTube and Spotify. Owning publishing is like having the master key to the music business. The one, who owns the publishing and copyright, is the one who wins. When you own enough publishing rights, then depending on the success of the songs you own, you could be earning passive income, for the rest of your life. Producer Daz Dillinger recently showed his quarterly publishing royalty statement totaling more than $193,000 from songs he made over 20 years ago with 2Pac and Dr. Dre. You can search the video on YouTube now. When the hype train slows down, publishing is where all your money will be. In 1985, Michael Jackson acquired ATV Music Publishing for $47.5 million dollars. Paul McCartney, who had told Jackson about the importance of owning publishing, admitted he felt somewhat undercut by the purchase, because ATV Music Publishing owned the publishing rights to most of The Beatles' songs, although McCartney did not enter the bidding when it came up for sale in 1984. This business move is another reason why Michael Jackson was one of the smartest and greatest music minds to ever live. In December 1995, Michael Jackson agreed to merge ATV Music Publishing with Sony Music Publishing, a division of Sony Corporation, to form Sony/ATV Music

Publishing. On March 14, 2016, Sony announced that it had reached a deal to acquire the Jackson estate's stake in the company for $750 million dollars. The deal was completed on September 30, 2016. When Dolly Pardon released her song "I Will Always Love You" in 1974, she had no way of knowing that pop star Whitney Houston would release a cover of her song in 1992, that would be part of the hugely successful "The Bodyguard" movie soundtrack. Whitney Houston's version of Dolly Pardon's song "I Will Always Love You" ended up becoming a bigger hit than Dolly's original version. Success stories like this is why publishing control is one of the most important aspects in the music business. Work as hard as you can to create great, timeless songs and protect your publishing interests with your life. Most people, who have signed co-publishing deals, regret it later on down the line. Imagine if you write a song that makes $1,000,000 and you own 100% of that song. The song may take a whole 12 months to generate the full one million dollars, so for 12 months, although you have a hit song, you are waiting for your publishing checks to start coming to your mailbox, or bank account, which doesn't happen until at least 9 months or more, after the song actually performed. You may be bankrupt at the time, and a publishing company may reach out to you by email and say, "Hey we want to give you some money for a partnership". The publishing company may be willing to advance you $100,000 against your $1,000,000 in future royalties, but when you split your publishing with the major publishing company, your $1,000,000 is now only $500,000, minus the $100,000 advance. So here is a situation where you could have earned a full one million dollars, but you took a $100,000 advance because you needed money now. Had you waited the 9-12 months, you would have received a full million dollars while still retaining 100% ownership. Now you're forced to split your publishing royalties with that major publishing company until the contract us over.   12 months later, after you have recouped the $100,000, and you look at your checks, you soon realize that your checks would have been double, had only you waited and not sold out half of your publishing for a silly $100k advance. Most time people are in financial binds, and they only think about having immediate cash in hand. They wont even bother reading the contract because all they'll be thinking about is leaving the publishing company's office with that $100,000 check. It's very tempting.   Now after four years, your song generates $6 million dollars total, you will only get $3 million in publishing. Most people would rather keep the full $6 million and that's why people often regret doing co-publishing deals.   On another note, you may be smart and use your publishing advance as an investment. With talent, you can buy better equipment and make more better quality hit songs, then retain your publishing on those new songs made with the advance money. Sometimes we need startup capital in business, so selling publishing shares for quick cash is always an option. I also like the association of being part of a major publishing company. Major publishing companies work on your behalf, as a songwriter, and do their best to keep your/their song catalog generating revenue. Major co-publishing companies will do their best to collect all of your royalties domestically and internationally. Being your own publisher is a job within itself and collecting royalties from around the World is no easy task for an un-established publishing company. Major publishing companies also hold annual award events for their songwriters, composers and publishing companies. If you have a hit song, you may be eligible for awards from your publishing company, which only adds more prestige to your resume. Winning awards gives you more leverage as a songwriter/composer and leverage is always good when negotiating future deals. That is a quick understanding of some of the pros and cons of signing a co-publishing deal.   I recently had a conversation with the owners of a new company called "Royalty Exchange", which is a company and website that gives songwriters and publishers the ability to auction their publishing shares, through online auctions (similar to eBay). Royalty Exchange says their auctions allow rightsholders to sell a portion of their royalties through an online bidding process with multiple buyers interested in alternative investment opportunities. Sellers can choose to retain control over their copyrights, and are not required to sell 100% of their royalty stake. The Royalty Exchange auctions are very fast and effective, from what I can see, and their service appears to be a great option for royalty owners looking to raise fast capital. Royalty Exchange claims that sellers will receive the fair market value for their works. Remember, you may regret selling your publishing later in life, so hold on to your publishing. Owning publishing is as great investment and it is very similar to owning a bunch of good real estate. Music continues to appreciate and you never know if your song will be used in the future. Use your best judgment when your publishing   rights   are   on   the   line.

11 WHAT'S A PRO?

A Performing Rights Organization (or PRO) helps songwriters and publishers get paid for the usage of their music by collecting one of the most important forms of publishing revenue: performance royalties. As a songwriter, composer, or lyricist, you're owed what is called a "performance royalty" any time your music is played on radio stations (terrestrial, satellite, and internet), used on TV shows or commercials, or performed in live venues. Performance royalties are paid by radio stations, venues, TV networks, movie studios and public institution where songs are played, to Performing Rights Organizations like ASCAP, BMI, SESAC, and SOCAN (in Canada) who then distribute the money to their affiliated songwriters and publishers.   Performing Rights Organizations collect performance royalties for publishers and songwriters. Performing Rights Organizations do not collect mechanical royalties, sync fees, digital performance royalties associated with the creation of a master recording. If you are a recording artist you will need to get a writers and publishers account with a PRO, if you would like to collect all of your royalties. Most songwriters make the mistake of only collecting their writer's share of the royalties and never bother to set up an LLC, which is needed to create a publisher's account with your PRO. If you don't collect your publishing royalties, then someone else will. Right now as I type this, there are multi-millions of dollars in unpaid publisher royalties, to writers who are obvious to money that they have waiting for them in escrow. All you need to do is set up a publishing company to collect your publishing royalties. You don't need to be a lawyer or you don't need to be a genius to do this. Follow the steps in Chapter 3 to set up an LLC and get a EIN Tax ID number. Once you have your LLC and Tax ID, you can then sign up for a publishers account with ASCAP and BMI. I have publishing companies with ASCAP and BMI. I originally signed up to ASCAP as a writer then soon afterwards; I set up a publishing company with ASCAP. I have two clients who were featured on an album that sold over a million records. One has a writer's account with ASCAP, the other has a writer's account with BMI. Both of them never bothered to set up a publishing company and they never collected their share of the publishing from that song on the platinum album. Between the both of them, I believed they had over $30,000 in unpaid royalties and they agreed to allow me to retrieve their unpaid funds. I already had a publishing company with ASCAP, so I was easily able to make a claim for the unpaid royalties for my ASCAP writer. I then had to set up a BMI publisher's account, so that I could collect royalties for my BMI writer. I now am the owner of two separate publishing companies. An ASCAP publisher cannot collect royalties on behalf of a BMI writer; therefore I had to set up another

LLC for my BMI publishing company. I can only imagine how many other artists around the world never bothered to set up an LLC, to claim their publishing shares. This is the definition of leaving money on the table. Don't let ignorance stop you from collecting the royalties that are owed to you. I suggest that you learn as much as you can about copyright, music publishing and royalties. There is another company called SoundExchange in which you can sign up to, to collect your Digital Performance Royalties. SoundExchange is an organization that collects royalties on behalf of sound recording copyright owners and artists for any non-interactive transmissions of their music via satellite radio (such as Sirius XM), Internet radio (such as Pandora), as well as cable TV music channels. SoundExchange royalties are not the same as the royalties you get from performing rights organizations such as ASCAP and BMI. SoundExchange pays artists and sound recording owners; ASCAP and BMI pay songwriters/composers and publishers. An interactive streaming service (also known as on-demand streaming) is a music service, which allows you choose the songs that are played. On an ISS you may rent music and start, stop, skip, or share it. Spotify, Rhapsody, Google Play, Apple Music are examples of interactive streaming services. ISS pay performance royalties & mechanical royalties for rights of reproduction. Non-interactive streaming services also known as Internet Radio are streaming services such as Pandora, Sirius XM, NPR are like terrestrial radio stations where listeners play music, without the ability to choose the songs that play next. Non-interactive streaming services generate performance royalties. These are performances like radio, but digital. Thus, terrestrial radio and other radio-like services generate only performance royalties. PROs are responsible for tracking and collecting performance royalties generated from terrestrial and Internet radio. We'll talk more about the different types of royalties in the next chapter.

12 ROYALTIES

There are several types of music royalties that you may receive. I'll try my best to describe them all and tell you how to make sure you are collecting all royalties for your musical compositions. 1. Performance Royalties - Performing right royalties are paid to songwriters and publishers whenever their songs are performed. It is based on a songwriter's and publisher's right to perform the work – or cause a sound recording to be heard – in public. Performance right royalties are paid on terrestrial radio plays of songs and songs played in clubs, in restaurants, in bars - anywhere music is played publicly. The royalties are also collected whenever someone does a cover version of their song. A performance-rights license allows music to be performed live or broadcast. These licenses typically come in the form of a "blanket license," which gives the licensee the right to play a particular PRO's entire collection in exchange for a set fee. Licenses for use of individual recordings are also available. All-talk radio stations, for example, wouldn't have the need for a blanket license to play the PRO's entire collection. The performance royalty is paid to the songwriter and publisher when a song is performed live or on the radio. 2. Mechanical Royalties - Mechanical royalties are paid to songwriters for the use of musical compositions for use on CDs, records, and tapes. A mechanical license refers to permissions granted to mechanically reproduce music onto some type of media such as cassette tape, CD, vinyl record, for public distribution. Payment is based on sales of the CDs, records or tapes. For instance, when a record label presses a CD of a song, a mechanical royalty payment is due to the songwriter. If the songwriter has a publishing deal, then the publisher gets a percentage of the songwriter's mechanical royalties. 3. Digital Performance Right - Digital Performance Right (DPR) is the right of the sound recording copyright owner to perform or cause his/her sound recording to be performed via digital transmission. DPR royalties are paid to record labels and performers for the performance of their sound records via digital transmissions, i.e. satellite TV and digital cable, non-interactive websites (including re-transmissions of terrestrial radio), interactive webcasting services, and satellite radio. 4. Synchronization (Sync) - Sync royalties are paid to copyrighted music that is paired with visual media of any kind, including films, commercials, and online/streaming video and advertisements. These royalties are often negotiated on the front end of the licensing process, and are paid based on how many times the song will be used, and for which audience. A synchronization license is needed for a song to be reproduced onto a television program, film, video, commercial, radio, or even an 800 number phone message. It is called this because you are "synchronizing" the composition, as it is performed on the audio recording, to a film, TV commercial, or spoken voice-over. If a specific recorded version of a composition is used, you must also get permission from the record company in the form of a "master use" license. The synchronization royalty is paid to songwriters and publishers for use of a song used as background music for a movie, TV show, or commercial. 5. Print Music - Print royalties are the simplest, and least common, form of payment that is paid to an artist. This type of royalty applies to copyrighted music that is transcribed to a print piece, like sheet music, and then distributed. Royalties are paid to the copyright holder based on the amount of copies made for the printed piece. Print music royalties were more common years ago, before the digital age. In addition to these royalties, the Audio Home Recording Act of 1992 brought about yet another royalty payment for songwriters and performers. This act requires that the manufacturers of digital audio recording devices and the manufacturers of blank recording media (blank cassette tapes, blank CDs, blank DVDs, etc.) pay a percentage of their sales price to the Register of Copyrights to make up for loss of sales due to the possible unauthorized copying of music. There are two funds set up where this money is funneled. One is the Sound Recording Fund, which receives two-thirds of the money. This money goes to the recording artist and record company. The other fund is the Musical Works Fund, which receives the remaining one-third of the money to split 50/50 between the publisher and the songwriter. Signing up to a PRO is key in collecting your domestic and international royalties. It would be nearly impossible for a sole individual to try to track and collect all of their royalties on behalf of themselves. PROs have partnerships with companies around the world, who use musical compositions, who then in turn, pay the PRO for the usage. One of the big sources of publishing revenue you'll earn as a songwriter is performance royalties. But an even bigger revenue stream (at least for the music publishing industry at large) is mechanical royalties. In the U.S., the Record Label is responsible for paying the songwriter a fixed mechanical royalty rate of $0.091 for each song sold. A simple example is if Ed Sheeran released a new 10 song album, which sells an even one million copies. The record label owes Ed $91,000 for letting them "publish" his 10 songs. Here is an example with two writers: Ed Sheeran writes a 10 song album with Taylor Swift and Taylor writes 80% of each song (Ed writes the other 20%). This album also sells one million copies. Here, Taylor is owed $72,800 and Ed is owed $18,200. Songwriter earnings are unpredictable and notoriously difficult to estimate. Without a detailed record of all record sales, downloads, streams, radio spins, and licenses to TV, films, and advertisements, it's impossible to know how much a song has earned.

13 THE RISE OF STREAMING

Streaming music services were for the first time ever responsible for more than 50% of all U.S. music industry revenue in 2016, according to new numbers released by the Recording Industry Association of America (RIAA) Thursday. Paid and ad-supported streaming together generated 51% of music revenue last year, to be precise, bringing in a total of $3.9 billion. In 2015, streaming music was responsible for 34% of the music industry's annual revenue. Much of that increase can be attributed to a strong growth of paid subscriptions to services like Spotify and Apple Music. Revenue from paid subscription plans more than doubled in 2016, bringing in $2.5 billion, with an average of 22.6 million U.S. consumers subscribing to streaming services last year. The year before, subscription services had an average of 10.8 million paying subscribers. In fact, in the first half of 2017, audio streams were up 58.5% and reached a new record high of 179.8 billion. Spotify's subscriber base is now 50 million+ and is already close to three times the size it was two years ago – and five times the size it was three years ago. Spotify announced last week that it now attracts over 140m monthly active users, around 53 million of which are believed to be paying subscribers. Apple announced earlier this month that it now has more than 27 million subscribers on its Apple Music streaming platform. In recent years, streaming income has eclipsed digital music downloads. The volume of subscription streams on the likes of Spotify and Apple Music jumped by more than 69% in the US during the first half of this year to 141.3 billion – dramatically outperforming the number of online music video streams in the same period. US-based music streams on online video services such as YouTube grew by just 6.1% to 101.5 billion in the first half of 2017, some 39.8 billion behind the total play count of on-demand subscription audio platforms. Ad-funded and subscription audio platforms attracted 179.8 billion on-demand streams in the January-June 2017 period, up 58.5% on the same period of 2016. Overall, audio streams took a 64% share of all on-demand music plays in the six months, with video streams on 36%. In the same period of 2016, video claimed a 46% share. What this data tells me is that year after year, people are catching up with technology and are accepting music streaming services as the premier destination for their consumption of music. A few years ago, streaming was frowned upon because the technology hadn't caught up with consumers and the payouts didn't seem worthwhile versus the financial opportunity that came with physical and digital music sales. That has all changed drastically over the last couple of years. Spotify now accounts for 69.6% of the major label's overall streaming revenues. Global recorded music revenues increased by 5.9%. Digital income now accounts for 50% of global music revenues. The huge growth in paid streaming led to a big decline in paid downloads, with iTunes and other transactional digital music services bringing in 22% less money in 2016, to the tune of $1.8 billion. CD sales also continued to fall, with all physical media bringing in $1.7 billion, which is 16% below 2015 levels. Any artist will tell you, that they would much rather have people downloading their songs or buying their CDs, because the artist will make more money, but the fact is, music isn't being consumed the same as it used to be and people are streaming more than they are downloading and buying physical albums. Spotify is the top paying streaming service yet they only pay an average of $0.004 per stream. That means if you do one million streams on Spotify, you will only be paid $4000 in royalties. In contrast, one million song downloads would generate around $1,000,000 dollars, if the downloads are $0.99 (before iTunes takes their 1/3 cut). There is no question that streaming music has been a major factor in the financial decline of the music business. Based on the statistics, we cannot deny that streaming has become the preferred choice of music consumption. At one point, pop music star Taylor Swift didn't want any of her music on Spotify. Swift recently doubled back on her strict stance against streaming platforms that allow users to listen entirely for free as she rejoined the masses by uploading her material onto Spotify. The vast majority of her back catalog had been missing for years, and for a while, it looked like she might never find her way back to the world's most popular streaming outlet. Taylor and her team are smart enough to see how the tides have changed and to know that if her music isn't available to the 150 million-plus listeners that Spotify has been able to attract, it will negatively affect whatever she does next. Streaming music and Spotify is simply too large and far too important these days to ignore, no matter what an artist feels about the compensation that streaming services pay.

14 WHAT HAPPENS WHEN YOU MAKE A HIT SONG?

When you make a hit song, and it starts gaining traction and momentum, your phone will start ringing nonstop. All of a sudden everyone will want to jump on the bandwagon and be part of your success. People who you probably never thought you would be in contact with, will start reaching out you, hoping to get a piece of the small fortune that you are about to accumulate. People try to pull you in every direction possible, so it's best that you and your team stay grounded. Don't make yourself so easily accessible either. If you made it this far, then you obviously have an email set up and this is probably the best form of contact. I say that because emailing people keeps you at a nice distance from them. They never truly know whose on the other end of the email, when you respond to them. They don't know if they're talking to you, your manager, your lawyer, or your mom. It's best to keep things this way. Lots of people will call you with nonsense and find ways of getting your number. Try your best not to entertain it all. Don't get caught up in too many phone conversations with random people either. It can be a big waste of time. People always have a lot to say, and people always talk a good one, when they are trying to get close to you. People will talk your ear off and want you to appear at this or that event, in order to help bring some of your buzz, their way. Don't fall for this.

Now that you have a hit song, it's time for you and your team to get paid. The only people that you need to be speaking to at this point are show promoters and booking agents. Show promoters are people who have built working relationships with several venues where you may be able to perform for a paid fee. Depending on how big your song is at the time, you may be getting offers anywhere from $500-$10,000 to perform. You will probably need a song in the Top 40 and below to demand show prices as high as $10,000 or more. Use your best judgment when agreeing to perform at venues. The goal is for you to make money and not spread yourself too thin. People will email you and ask you, "how much is your performance rate". Never respond with a set number. Always ask what their first offer is, first. That way you can gauge if you'd even like to continue communication with that person. You may be setting your bar too low, and underestimating your value, so it's always good to get a general idea of what your different offer prices are. Partnering with a booking agency may be your best bet. When my first music project was at it's height, some of the top booking agents were flying out to have meetings with us. If booking agents aren't reaching out to you, then maybe you need to continue building your buzz. A booking agent will not reach out to you unless they are aware of your brand. Emailing a booking agent that is not interested in booking you, does not work, from my experience. Booking agents only want to deal with the hottest acts. Their goal is to book you at the highest rates so that they can take their 10% booking fee. If your are only demanding $500 per show, then it's probably not worthwhile for a booking agent, because they'd only be receiving $50 per show, which is peanuts to them. Handling your own bookings is the best route to take before you reach the next level. Your next goal would probably be to continue building your buzz until a more known artist wants you to open up for their show dates. In that case, you may be only getting $1000 per show, but if it is a tour with 10-30 dates, you could easily generate $10k-$30k, in a month or two. Allowing opportunities to happen organically is the best way to do it in my opinion. Being hasty and seeming thirsty, is a big turn off for most people. Be humble with your songs success and continue to build your buzz until it really pays off. Try not to get too excited and stay humble. If someone makes an offer for you to perform and it is too low, then respectfully decline. Never respond in an arrogant way and never feel disrespected by low offers. Promoters are in the business to make a profit also and at times you may have to compromise. Some venues are small and the promoters can only generate a certain amount in sales, based off your buzz. Find out what your best offer is, and find out your lowest offer. That way you will have a good idea of your performance value. Booking too many shows at a low rate can damage opportunities of getting paid more in the future. I've found that in the promoting world, some promoters are in contact with each other promoters, and they refer to each other to find out what a specific artist has charged for booking in the past. That is why it's best to figure out your maximum value before you make a bunch of obligations to lower paying shows. Your booking price can go up over night, so it's best to only book the highest paying shows. Some artists are very eager to perform in front of a live audience but you must not be too hasty. Remember, if you are getting 1000 streams a day on YouTube, it's not much different than performing in front of 1000 people at a show. Performing in front of people is a good way to get your brand out there, but I think it's better to be efficient. If you can get a booking agent to cover your travel and hotel expenses, that's even better. If a promoter gives you an offer and uses the term "all in", then that means you will have to cover the cost of your travel and hotel. You may find that after paying for a flight, taxi, hotel and food, you may be breaking even. This is not worth your time. If you get an "all in" offer, never book a show without considering the price of flights, hotel and travel costs. You may be breaking If you and your team aren't making a profit, then it defeats the purpose in traveling somewhere to perform. Like I said, you can reach plenty of people daily, by simply putting content on YouTube often. You don't need to be in anyone's face, to build your brand. Make sure it's worth your while. The bigger your song gets, you may start receiving calls from old friends or people you may have known in the past. This is natural. Some people may be calling just to say hello and acknowledge that they see you succeeding, others will find it as an opportunity to try to get something out of you. You may have not received your first royalty yet, but the public perception may be that you are rich, because you have a viral video or a song on the radio. Stay clear of anyone who seems to be an opportunist, looking to use you for your new success. Some people will genuinely be happy and proud of your success, others will really start acting fake and start to despise you. You must be very careful, as you get closer to ultimate success. This is usually when you will start experiencing the most turmoil and will have to decide who your real friends and family are. Having a hit song is similar to winning the lottery. People will feel that just because they know or knew you at some point in life, that they have some entitlement to your future income. Stay clear of anyone looking to come up off of you. If they weren't there when you were struggling to build your brand, then they need to continue to stay on the sidelines. There is nothing wrong with being an inspiration to people and accepting the blessings that people may send your way, but do not let people infiltrate your organization. These are the worst types of people.

Most times, people don't want to help bake the cake, but they want a piece of it when it comes out the oven and that isn't fair to you as the baker. You're the one who had to gather the flour, the eggs, the milk, the heat for the stove. You're the one who even thought to make a cake and spent the time mixing the ingredients to make the cake batter. It's not fair for someone to show up, after the cake is baked, with his or her plate out. Don't get caught up with these types of people. You must also learn to divert requests that people may ask you, to someone else in your team (even if that person doesn't exist). For years, anytime someone would call my business line, I'd never admit that they were speaking to me, the owner of the company, I would always say my name is "Tai", the head of customer service. Don't give people the benefit of thinking they are talking to the boss. Always make it seem like they must go through different channels to reach the boss. You can't call the Facebook hotline and reach Mark Zuckerberg. Keep it like this for your business, even if you don't have many employees. This will always create the impression that your organization is bigger than it really is. People tend to have more respect for big businesses. ALWAYS make it seem as if you are NOT the point person to contact. If you have a problem saying no to people, always say, "I will have to talk to my team and get back to you about that". This way, you divert the pressure off of yourself and you direct it to the unknown. Directing people to the unknown, keeps them off balance, leaving them without a conclusion. When you leave someone to no conclusion, then it keeps them interested and it makes them want to get to the bottom of the situation, which you will never allow them. When people feel like they know you or they can easily reach you, they may try to do whatever they can to take advantage. This business is all about you being at the full advantage. Keep your advantage.   Be as hard to reach as you possibly can. Surround yourself in an air of mystery. Try your best not to respond to everyone. Some people will reach out to you, with no business at all, just to see if they can get a response or get in contact with you. This is why they call it the "music game". You win the game by keeping people off balance. No one should be able to predict your next move. Being hasty to respond to people will only make you seem regular to them. True celebrities are not easy to reach. If it were easy to reach Beyoncé, then she wouldn't be Beyoncé. You can't just pick up the phone and get Tom Cruise on the line. Create a space between you and whoever is reaching out to you. Remember, if someone is emailing or calling you, they are already interested in you. You keep people interested in you by not being interested in them. You're supposed to be busy working on great music and art, instead of worrying about what some guy in an email is talking about.

Don't be so fast to give people what they want from you. Some people are just looking for the satisfaction in knowing that they have some sort of control of you, whether it's you picking up the phone when they call or responding to their email in a fast manner. Don't let anyone get the upper hand on you. Don't give anyone the satisfaction of feeling as if they "got you". People like to pursue. Let them pursue you. Never be an easy catch. Never fall for their bait.   Nowadays, everyone is on the Twitter, Facebook, Snapchat, Instagram, etc.. and it's devaluing what a celebrity really is. A celebrity is someone who is celebrated. Let people celebrate you and leave it at that. People should never feel like they can touch you. The minute that you can be touched is the minute that people start looking at you as a regular mortal human being. Remember, you are not regular any more, you have created a hit song. You are now in an elite club of artists and hitmakers. Communicate with other elite people who can bring value to your situation. If people are not bringing value to your brand, then they are taking away from it. You do not need to respond to everyone. Leave people wondering if you even read their email. They'll email you again later, and continue to pursue you. When they finally do reach you, they will feel like they had to work to get to you, and that is the distance that you need to keep. No one ever respects the easy slut girl that shares her vagina with everyone at school. Most men desire women who seem out of their league and they're often intimidated to even speak to them. I remember when my artist became famous and had a hit song, and then all of a sudden, he had all of these new "friends". I frowned upon it, yet I let him do his own thing. I knew that this would be part of his downfall. He seemed like a lonely person before the success and he was embracing all of the new people that were coming in his life. Meanwhile, all of these people were using the buzz that I helped to create, but not bringing any real value back to our business. Next thing I knew, we couldn't go anywhere without 10 people following behind us. I remember once, we were going to an event, and I called two SUVs to come pick us up. We couldn't even all fit in the two trucks because he had a gang of people that just wanted to tag along. It was disgusting. I'm personally at the point in my life where I don't need any new friends, unless they are helping to bring some sort of value in my life. These people will come and go as soon as your song starts to die down. Stay away from people do not care about your true well-being. Be very careful of who you bring into your circle. It can be your downfall.

15 GETTING A RECORD DEAL… OR DO YOU REALLY NEED ONE?

If you follow all the rules in this book, you may have several record labels calling your phone looking to sign you or your act. Being independent is really a blessing, if you are fortunate enough to be able to generate monthly revenue from your music and pay your bills. Any deal that you sign will come with some sort of compromise. If you aren't willing to compromise, then you shouldn't get into agreements with other people and other businesses. When you are independent, you really cannot fail. Any profit made, is a win. You become somewhat of a slave to the label when you owe them millions of dollars. I personally would not want to owe anyone millions, unless I was 100% sure that I could generate it back. Think about this. Would you rather take $2 million dollars and owe someone, or would you rather earn $2 million dollars on your own time and not owe anyone? This is what you must consider before signing a record deal. Are you mentally in the position to handle a large amount of money and is your brand strong enough to make the labels investment in you worthwhile? You must think about this before you sign a deal because if things don't go as planned, you could end up at the record label's mercy.

You have to use your best judgment before signing a recording contract. Upon signing a record deal, you are typically giving up rights and control of your music. Usually you give up a percentage of control in your master recordings, copyright, publishing and often times, you may be giving up some creative control. Record companies aren't just giving you money because they like you, they are loaning you money to create a project, with hopes of them earning a profit on the money they loaned you. If you ever hear an artist say, "they got an advance", that means that a record label loaned that artist some money to produce new projects. New pressure also comes with signing with a major label. If you don't live up to the expectations of your success, it may compromise your brand. The media tends to like to see people failing and if your sales aren't impressive, harsh writers may call you a "flop" or a "one hit wonder", which could alter people's perception of you or your brand. Let's say you have a nice Internet buzz, and then you sign a record deal with a label. You then release your album and it doesn't perform as well as people expected. Most major labels would then remove you from the priority list and may not invest any more money into your promotion, and try to cut their losses as slim as possible. Record labels aren't going anywhere and the labels will continue to keep an eye out for you, as long as you keep making the right moves. Once label offers are available, they usually stay on the table as long as you can continue to maintain your buzz. Never rush to sign a record deal. If the label is interested enough in taking a risk on you, then you are doing something right and you should probably continue to do what it is that you are doing to succeed.

If you are new to the business and your company or artist hasn't demonstrated a long track record of success, then major record labels may offer you a $50,000-$150,000 recording advance with a 4 or 5 album recording deal varying anywhere from $1 million to $5 million dollars. When you sign a million dollar record deal, that doesn't mean the record company writes you a check for a million dollars. A multi-million dollar recording deal means that the label agrees to allocate a multi-million dollar budget, for the recording of your future album releases. You will be obligated to recoup all of the money that the label spends on the costs of recording your project.   Record labels are like any bank. If you have a successful business, then it may be wise to get a small business loan to advance your operations. If you aren't a successful business, then you may not be ready for a loan and may not have built up enough credit for the banks to even consider giving you a loan. When your credit is excellent, you can always get a loan. So never feel rushed to sign on the first loan that a bank offers. Do your research; find the best annual percentage. This works the same in the music business.   One of the mistakes I've personally made in life is overusing too much of my credit, before I established enough sources of income. Many people make this mistake and are in debt for that reason. 80% of Americans are in debt. Most artists who sign record deals have never had any real money and have never cashed a $50k-$100k check. Some artists make the mistake of spending their recording advance on cars, jewelry, clothes, nice apartments, women and whatever you can image. This is typical behavior of someone who has been poor most of their life, and then all of a sudden comes into a small fortune. Remember, the label gave you that money to invest in your music production. This is why staying independent may be better for some people. You tent to be more careful with your own money. When you feel as if you're spending someone else's money, then some people are more frivolous. But again, that is the misconception that most artists have after singing a record deal. They believe they are using the labels money but they are really spending their own money. The label wont advance you a dime that they wont recoup before you get paid again.   Some people want to be signed to a record label for the affiliation. Affiliate yourself by being successful in your field and not by being a bandwagon rider.

Don't get caught in the hype of being signed to the same label as your favorite artist. Just because you may sign to the same label as Justin Bieber, doesn't mean you two are going to be best friends nor does it mean that you will achieve the same amount of success as him. The best thing you can do is build your brand organically and make great music. Fans don't magically appear and if they do, they wont last if you aren't bringing anything new to the table. If you are doing the right things, other people/artists will automatically want to be affiliated with you and your brand. I found that it's best not to pursue people. Let people pursue you. Record labels can also help with promoting you and getting your brand in places you may have neglected but don't put too much confidence in a record label. Go to any major label website and see how many artists that they have signed. I'd bet half of the artists that you see, you have never heard of them. All artists who are signed to a major record label are not successful. Signing to a record label can be helpful if you and your team have always established a winning formula. Do not depend on the label to make you succeed. The label is just there for support. You must take your career into your own hands.

16 STAYING RELEVANT

Staying relevant is like going to the gym and working out everyday. Going to the gym to watch other people workout wont get you in shape. You must workout on your own and if you want to see results then you must workout a few times a week. Creating buzz and relevance online is exactly the same. You must be releasing content at least once a week, just like you would need to be in the gym at least once a week, if you'd like to stay in shape. The more days that you're working out at the gym, the faster you will start seeing results. There is no quick or easy way to remain relevant, besides constantly creating new content. True relevance means thousands of people are searching for you, on a daily basis. If no one is searching for you, then you are irrelevant. Don't feel bad about it, just create content that will get people talking and searching for you or your brand.

If you were fortunate enough to create a hit song or successfully launch a viral marketing campaign, then congratulations. You are creating emotion stirring content. At this point, you must continue to create. There is never time to bask in the glory of your success. There is often a small window of opportunity or what some people would call "15 minutes of fame" and you must work to get past this phase. Use your new income and notoriety to create newer and better content. You may now understand how viral marketing works, and you may feel as if you can repeat the process over and over again. Once you figure out the process, it becomes easy. Never get comfortable and always stay creative. Do not let financial limitations stop you from creating. You must keep pushing your campaigns forward and repeat the success process. It is up to you to come up with great ideas for new compelling content, so I suggest that you always have brainstorming sessions with your team, where you all come up with content ideas and marketing campaigns that will work to keep your brand relevant. Don't be the person who is content with the minimal level of success. You must always find new ways to build your fan base. You must stay relevant if you want to reach your highest potential in the entertainment business.

I once managed an artist who would always go to other people's red carpet events just to stand on the red carpet and take photos. I wanted to shoot some new content with this artist, but she'd always be too busy socializing at other people's parties and events. One day I asked her, "Why did she feel the need to be at every event?". She told me, "She's keeping herself relevant.". I couldn't agree with her because it had been months since we put out any new and relevant content, on her behalf.

I don't believe that going to parties and being seen at the club all the time, truly keeps you relevant in the entertainment world. As a new artist or label, I would not recommend trying to be a socialite, as a way of staying relevant. People who are considered socialites are able to attend VIP parties and take red carpet photos because they are often from wealthy families and they don't really need to shoot new content to be famous because their fame is inherited. The goal is to be the conversation of the party and you don't need to be at the party to be the conversation. From my experience, putting out new content is the only true way to stay relevant. You can only physically be at one place at any given time. Your music and video content has the ability to be seen all over the world at any given time.

Going to celebrity parties and being spotted on red carpets may have been impressive before the digital age, but it really doesn't mean much anymore. With social media, everyone has access to where the hottest parties will be and anyone can be in the same club or party with their favorite celebrity with the help of Snapchat or Instagram. Instead of being an artist, and working on her art, this artist I worked with, was being a groupie and a bandwagon rider. True artists are creating new art and don't have time to be at everyone else's events. Create your own events and have people come to you. Be the talk of the party and not just another face at a party. Anyone can take a picture on a red carpet. Focus on your craft and don't get so caught up with what everyone else is doing. When you're busy chasing other people around, that's when you become irrelevant.

If you've ever read the book "The 48 Laws of Power" by Robert Greene you'd know that Law 16 says "Use Absence to Increase Respect and Honor". 48 Laws of Power also says "Too much circulation makes the price go down: The more you are seen and heard from, the more common you appear. If you are already established in a group, temporary withdrawal from it will make you more talked about, even more admired. You must learn when to leave. Create value through scarcity. Conversely, when you become too present, too accessible, leaving no room for the imagination, the more you pursue, the less they love you. What withdraws, what becomes scarce, suddenly seems to deserve our respect and honor. What stays too long, inundating us with its presence, makes us disdain it.".

That statement is the essence of what staying relevant in the digital media age is all about. Create relevance by being a prolific content creator. If not, then you will be in the mercy of other people, to keep you relevant, which usually doesn't work. If people aren't talking about you, then you probably aren't giving them anything to talk about. When you releasing content that people like, they will talk about it. People want and need new entertaining content and you must give the people what they want. The amount of people who are fed content far outweigh the amount of people who feed the content. Be a content feeder and don't bother being a bandwagon rider.

I've watched many artists get upset with bloggers and magazine writers for not writing articles about them. No blog is obligated to post your content and magazine writers don't need to write about you just because you released a new project. Understand that no one is looking to "put you on". The days of getting discovered in the mall by some music exec is over. Major labels, magazines and blogs keep their eyes on independent acts who are self sufficient. When these acts build a true loyal following and start selling out local shows, magazines and blogs have no choice but to pay attention to their movement. Your job is to attract fans, while not worrying about attracting major record labels, magazine writers and bloggers. Realize that it's no one else's job to keep you or your brand relevant, besides you and your team. Don't get caught up in what your favorite websites, magazines or blogs are doing. I found that most writers and bloggers are rarely trendsetters, so don't expect them to do anything for you or to "break" your content first. Most smaller blogs will only support what other mainstream publications post. Mainstream magazines are no different. Most magazine writers will only write about whatever is popular at the time and they have no interest in the unknown. Don't get upset with the writers and bloggers because you aren't making content that they want to support. When you create real buzz and relevance, the word will get out. Social media influence and word-of-mouth is usually the main contributing factors that will make magazine writers and bloggers write about you. I found that most bloggers usually have their own agenda and they're probably trying to break their own brands and artists through their blog outlet, so they have no interest in supporting anyone who wont bring their website or blog new traffic.

Everyone in the entertainment business is looking for relevance, not just you. Most people in the industry are like blood sucking vampires who are looking for people with fresh buzz and relevance to suck dry. People will become interested in you when they see you are accomplishing success and pulling off impressive marketing feats. Admiration is what gets people talking and writing about you. Make people admire you for your creative work and you will always be relevant.

I also noticed that people now seem more concerned about having followers than actually having content. People are even going so far as to pay for fake followers on social media sites, so that it appears as if they have a large fan base. I guess they assume that if they appear relevant, by boasting a large fake following, real people will eventually want to follow them. This method of social media marketing is a big waste of time. The goal isn't to appear relevant. The goal is to actually be relevant. Don't get so caught up in what other people think of your low social media follower count. This is a backwards approach. Your following will gradually go up, if you are creating and sharing relevant content. Having a bunch of followers means nothing if you have no content or products to offer.

If your goal is to be a social media personality and you have no music to sell, then you better find something to sell soon. A large social media following can also enable you to sell advertising to companies looking to advertise. If advertising is your goal then be clear that advertising is your product.

Create a service or have information to offer people, in your posts. There's millions of people on social media nowadays and people only want to follow other's who have something to offer. I've seen artist's followings increase from nearly nothing to tens of thousands of followers overnight. When you finally create something that people want to spread, your following will go up naturally and you wont have to pay for fake followers on your social media pages. When you have 100,000 fake followers, then you put out a song and nobody buys it, those fake fans will mean nothing. I'd rather have 100 real followers than 10,000 fake followers, any day.

Don't be a cheat and recognize that in order to get to the front of the line, sometimes you have to wait and be patient. Everyone in the business wants to get to the front of the line and anyone who thinks that they can skip the line, is despised. I've recently came across some YouTube creators who focus on what they call a "100 Day Challenge", where they post a new video everyday for 100 days. This method seems to work well as a way of building up a subscriber base. I'd recommend studying Google Trends and uploading relevant videos every day. I've also read that Google/YouTube rewards you with better search engine ranking when you upload relevant content frequently. Stay in the loop and build a large following of over a million fans. At that point, you become your own media outlet and you can never be irrelevant when you have over a million real fans.

17 THE ONE HIT WONDER

Nearly half of all musicians that created a chart hit in the half-century in between 1955 and 2005 never did so again – 47.5 percent, to be exact. The "one hit wonder" is an artist who makes a hit song, that reaches the music charts, then after their initial success, they never are able to outdo their prior success by making another hit song. If you are blessed enough to make a hit song and possibly make enough money to help take care of yourself and your family, then by all means, it's a blessing. Most people will never make a song that charts. One hit song can change your life forever. Depending on how big the hit song is, you may never need to make another hit song. There are plenty of artists still touring due to hit songs that they've made years and years ago. I can name dozens of examples. I'm sure you may know a few also. Some big hit songs even become a part of popular culture and continue to live on forever due to their repeated usage. Some radio stations focus solely on hits from the past. Older hit songs are also often used in television commercials, movies and TV shows. Other hit songs may be sampled by producers or remade by current artists. All you need is one good song, and you could be receiving royalties for the rest of your life, considering that you didn't give up all of your publishing rights to your song. If you skipped to this Chapter, we talk more about publishing in Chapter 10.

The goal of getting in the music business is to have a catalog of hit songs. Not just one hit song. True success in the music business, is having a large catalog of successful records under your belt. That is the ultimate end goal in this business.

Why do some artists have big songs and very successful years in the music business, and then all of a sudden, you don't hear from them anymore? They never seem to be able to follow up and make another smash record. Why is that? In my opinion, you have to stay hungry and humble, but that is a hard feat to accomplish, when you aren't actually hungry anymore. You can usually hear the raw emotion in good artist's music. It seems to me like artists create the best music, when they are under pressure, poor, desperate and have nothing to lose. When you take away those factors, then the music often suffers. Money and success may cause their songs to come across less emotional, or less real to common people who may be dealing with the same emotions that the artist may been going though, prior to their success.

Songs are usually about love, relationships or problems people go through in their lives. Money has a way of eliminating certain problems in people's lives. Have you ever noticed that most artists' best work is usually their first record, or their earlier works? I don't think it's a coincidence. I think with new money and success comes, less drive, less motivation, less creativity and sometimes arrogance. This doesn't happen to all artists. Some people don't allow money to misguide them. But those that do, usually end up becoming "one hit wonders".

I'd say 10 out of 10 hit songs are collaborative efforts. It's rare and near impossible to make a hit song solely by yourself. You will need at least a small team of 3-5 people to get your music brand to the level, to where you have a hit song that's playing on the radio or doing millions of streams online. I can't think of a music producer, who also happens to be a songwriter, an artist, who also knew how to record and mix themselves, while also being good in business and knowing how to run a their own record label, while marketing their song and having enough money to spend where needed, while also being a good graphic designer and web developer. It takes a team to make a hit song. You won't be able to pull all of this off on your own. I can't think of anyone who has done this all on their own. If anyone says, "they made it on their own", then they're lying to you. There are some businesses in which you may be able to run and be successful, without needing anyone but yourself. The music business is not one of them.

Be prepared to build a team of people, with similar goals, who will help you push your music brand. If you and your team are successful enough to make one hit song, then I would suggest staying with that team and attempting to repeat the process, over and over again. If you struck gold while digging a hole, would you continue digging in the same spot, or would you switch hole locations? If it were I, I'd put my flag at the hole where I found gold, and I'd keep digging. After that, if I kept digging and digging only to realize there's no more gold in that spot, then I would leave for a new hole. Build a team of winners and learn to win together. Think of a good team as being similar to a track team. When a track team is running a relay race, every runner on the team has to play their part and do their best. You can't expect to be able to run the whole relay race by yourself. That's what your team is there for. Know when to pass the baton to your teammates. You will burn yourself out, and you will lose if you tried to run a whole relay race on your own. Especially when you are running against other established teams, which may even outnumber you in runners.

I think the main reason why artists become one hit wonders, is because they choose to switch teams too soon. Be loyal and have faith in your team. It took at least ten people for me to make my first hit song. There was me as manager, writer, graphic designer, videographer, my brother helped with the marketing and strategy, the artist, who wrote and performed the song, two producers who created the music behind the song and another artist, who already had a huge following. Then we also had two separate sound engineers for the separate vocal recordings. I can't forget the graphic designer who made the artwork and my lawyer who helped us negotiate the record deal. I'm not even mentioning the major label and the various people who helped along the way such as the radio DJs, the bloggers who reposted our content, personal advisors, friends and family.

You will need to affiliate yourself with as many people as possible to help push your brand. You also need to maintain good relationships with all of these people, involved in your career. This is your team and you will only win with them. A small label isn't much different than a NBA team. Michael Jordan or LeBron James would not have won championships, if it were just them playing alone on the court. You will need at least five players on the court and five on the bench.

You may be the face of the brand but don't allow your new fame to neglect your team. Your team may be very important in the longevity of your success. Any problems that may arise, due to working with many people, you must try your best to work out internally. If your team starts to turn against you, then your career may be on the line. Now, in the social media era, when people are disgruntled, they tend to turn to social media to voice their discontent. You don't want anyone talking bad about you and you especially don't want your team to have any loose links. Remember, loose links sink ships! Do your best to resolve issues amongst each other, internally. If you do what's right for you and your team, then everyone will be happy and you all will grow and succeed.

The last artist that I managed became a one hit wonder after I worked for three years to make his career a success. After we made the hit song, he allowed his new fame and money to cloud his judgment. Immediately, after making the hit song, he was interested in working with a new management team. He didn't even give me a shot to help him deliver more hit songs, using my proven methods. He seemed to have thought that he had won the game, all on his own and disregarded and took for granted everything we had done for him. At the advice of my lawyer (which was tortious interference), we took a meeting with this "big management firm" who manages some major EDM (electronic dance music) acts. They had an office in Manhattan and they also had offices in Los Angeles and London. The meeting went well and they were very knowledgeable about the music business but I was not interested in working with them. I believe in the saying, "if it's not broke, then don't fix it". We were doing fine as a small boutique label/publishing firm, and things were only about to get better for us, as a unit, now that we had a hit song on the radio featuring Drake. I was never trying to hold the artist back and I wanted him to have the freedom to work with whomever he chose. I was willing to split my 20% management commission with the new management team, 50/50. I decided to make this sacrifice with hopes that this new team could deliver and make us a fortune, while I laid back, collected my royalties and continued to develop new artists for the label that I started with the artist, where we would then split the label profits 50/50. My trust in the artist was a big mistake and I highly undervalued my own role in the whole situation. I was playing the role as his record label and I failed by only signing the artist to a management agreement, when in fact, I was more than just a manager. The fact is, I was entitled to more than 20% management commission, yet I felt it was a fair commission, as long as my artist continued to do the right thing.

All we had to do was make more hit songs, yet the artist felt that he wanted to jump ship and work with this new management team. He didn't even know these guys at all. Their nice office must have impressed him. I am not easily impressed. We didn't even get a chance to get our own swanky office before he decided to abandon the situation that we helped him grow for the past 3 years.

At the time, I only had him signed to a management agreement, instead of a recording or publishing agreement, so I took a major loss in the long run. This was one of my biggest regrets, not signing him to a recording or publishing agreement. He then started working with this new management team behind my back. Like I said before, I was willing to split my 20% management commission with the new management team but the new management team came back and told me that they were only willing to give me 5% and they would keep the other 15%! I thought this was absurd because I still had another two years to manage him, according to our contract. They were attempting a hostile takeover and the fact was that I built the brand and project from scratch and was entitled to at least 50% of the business overall. They were crazy for even thinking that I would consider taking 5% when I know for a fact this artist would still be poor and unemployed if I didn't invest my time and knowledge into his project. If he could have done it all on his own, without me, then he would have already did it and I would have never even been in the equation from the start.

I was set to appear at the Grammy Awards in 2015, but when it was time to go to the awards show, I didn't hear from my artist. We spoke on FaceTime days before and he wasn't even man enough to tell me what his real plans were. The day of the 2015 Grammy Awards, I was faced with huge disappointment, realizing I was not going to the Grammy Awards for a song that I had 110% involvement in. The next day, I saw pictures and video footage of him on the Grammy Awards Red Carpet with one of the guys from the new management team that was at the meeting we had. I thought to myself, "wow, he really abandoned his team and stabbed us in the back". It made no sense for me to accept 5%, so at this point, I started putting my lawsuit together.

One of my roles as manager was helping the artist decide which songs to record, and which songs not to record. At times, I'd also help the artist come up with melodies and song ideas. When re-recording old songs, I would sometimes remind him of parts from the old recordings, that he may have forgotten to use on the new records. I played a major role in quality control, taste and selection of his music. My brother also was a second ear for me and would give me constructive critical opinions, which help to mold the finished product. The artist was talented artist, but he had raw talent, which needed shaping and molding. Without us, his music lacked certain elements.

Under the new management, he then started to release a string of horrible songs and albums, which never surpassed the hit song that we'd made together as a team. He really had the opportunity to fall back and plan for his next big hit, but he did the exact opposite. He released bad song after bad song and even started working with artists, who in my opinion, were below him. I had plans to link him with bigger and more legendary artists such as Stevie Wonder, who happens to be good friends with my uncle Edwin Birdsong, but that plan never happened. I had really big plans for this artist and at the time, he was the hottest new artist in the music business. He soon ruined that and continued to release horrible records, which never charted. At that point, I filed a lawsuit against him and the new management team for tortious interference and breach of contract among other things. I'm sure his music and creativity were also affected by the stress that came with the lawsuit.

I settled my lawsuit with him and ended up taking a major loss. Meanwhile, he was doing nothing but shaming himself and us. He hasn't had another hit song, since we worked with him. The artist even went so far as to slander me, because his personal plans, after stabbing us in the back, didn't seem to work out. That's usually how karma works. I'm waiting to see if he will make another hit song, but the odds are highly against him, more than ever. All I can do is imagine what would have happened, had he continued to work with his team, instead of having doubts. The new management company wasn't able to do anything creative for him besides put their hand in his pocket while reaping the benefits of our three years of work on his project. This sort of company is good with operational management, but they lack skills in creative management.

Stick with the people who you worked with to gain your initial success, or this may happen to you. Eventually, everyone has to go their separate ways, in life and in business, but don't abandon your team for "pie in the sky" when you have pie in your hands already.

To this day, I'm still puzzled as to why he decided to jump ship when his project was in it's prime. He must have thought the grass was greener on the other side. It's usually not and this was the perfect example. I recently heard that he parted with the new management team after two years of working with them, to no real success. They were never able to replicate or outdo the success that we created, with the small team that we had. His career has officially gone down the hill and he is what you would call a "one hit wonder".

I hear about these types of stories all the time and that is why one hit wonders are common. People with no true core values often allow money and fame to change them into disgusting people. Usually when an artist becomes famous, new people get in their ear and try to persuade them in other directions. If the artist is weak minded, disloyal and has no consideration for their team, then their careers usually start to go downhill afterwards. Things usually start going bad, when you are closest to success. A good team may only come once in a lifetime, so remember, loyalty over royalty. No one wants to work with a person who isn't a team player, and you will need a core team to continuously make hit records. So no matter how talented you may think you are as an individual, you will not make it in this business on your own. Teamwork makes the dream work.

In other instances, I see artists who mold their whole career around sounding like another popular artist. This usually doesn't work out well in the long run. There is an artist named Desiigner who came out in 2016 with a hit song called "Panda". The tone of Desiigner's voice and style of rapping sounded identical to another rapper named Future. When I first heard the "Panda" song, I thought I was listening to Future, but it was actually Desiigner. The "Panda" song became a huge hit and it was one of the biggest hit songs of 2016. The ironic part of it all was that Future had never had a hit song, bigger than "Panda". Someone had actually made a bigger song than Future ever did, using his own style and voice. I'm sure that didn't sit too well with Future, but at this point, it doesn't seem like Desiigner will be able to repeat the process. I think the buzz around the "Panda" song was centered around the fact that people thought it was Future. Once people realized that it was not a Future song, and it was really just a copy cat artist, his buzz started to decline. I'd bet the farm that Desiigner will never have a hit song bigger than "Panda". His career is on the decline and this is the reason why you can't expect to have a long career by sounding like someone else. There is nothing new under the sun, but you must at least make some sort of effort to be original. There was another artist named "Shyne" who got a record deal simply because his voice sounded almost identical to the late rapper Notorious B.I.G. aka Biggie Smalls. Shyne had a few hit song and had some buzz surrounding him due to sounding like Biggie, but his career was short lived.

Some would argue that making a hit song is a mere "accident" but I don't believe that's true. From my experience, to make it on the charts, there has to be some sort of planning and calculation. In previous chapters I speak about copying and finding inspiration from other people's work. There is nothing wrong with being inspired by other people's creations but try your best not to build a career around being a blatant copycat. I'm not saying what Desiigner did was completely wrong. Do whatever it takes to win, as long as it's not foul play. If you don't want to be a one-hit-wonder and are looking for longevity in the music business, then I'd suggest adding some of your own originality to the equation. These are just some of my personal opinion and you must do whatever works best for you, to succeed. The best advice I can give is for you to have faith in your team, be prolific and be as original as possible, if you don't want to end up a one-hit-wonder.

18 EXIT STRATEGY

No matter how successful you become in the music business, I believe one should always diversify. Once you make a substantial amount of money in the music business, it may be time for you to figure out what your other passions are in life. There are many different businesses that you can start to generate income. You must figure out what you are good at and what makes sense for you. Create as many income-generating businesses as possible, while you have the money to do so. Don't wait until your music checks start drying up before deciding that you need to create another source of income. One idea would be to find an already successful product that you like and make your own version of the product with your own branding. If you were able to build a successful music brand, then you're probably capable of successfully selling almost anything. Most of the very successful musicians diversified and used their music following to start acting careers, market clothing lines, beverages, do public speaking and start all sorts of successful businesses outside of music. Hip Hop mogul Russell Simmons used the fortune he made from founding Def Jam Records in 1983, to start RushCard in 2003. RushCard is a prepaid debit card company in which Russell sold to GreenDot for $147 million in 2017. This is a great example of turning music money into unimaginable fortunes, by diversifying.

Reinvest the money you make in the music business, back into yourself. Use the revenue that you make from music to buy newer and better equipment so that you can make better music. Avoid investing your profits in frivolous possessions like cars, clothes, jewelry and other toys. You can reinvest in yourself by buying a better computer, buying a better microphone, buying real estate and opening studios or whatever ideas your mind can come up with. The goal is to stay active and to constantly keep building. Mark Wahlburg is another great example of someone who took his fame from music, diversified his career and made a fortune. Mark started his career in the early 90s as rapper "Marky Mark". Mark then got into acting and went on to become one of Hollywood's most recognized faces. In recent years, Mark partnered with his brothers to start a successful burger franchise called "Wahlburgers", which also has it's own cable TV reality show on A&E of the same name. Wahlburgers restaurants have become a huge success and they are set to open 118 new locations over the next five to seven years. In 2013, Mark announced that he would be partnering with Sean "Diddy" Combs to launch a new alkaline water brand "AQUAhydrate". AQUAhydrate is now one of the top contenders in the bottled alkaline water sector and is sold in stores Worldwide.

Don't let music be the end plan. Music has always been a great way of reaching people and bringing people together. Use this to your advantage. Always have as many products and brands to pitch, as possible. The music business is highly based on you being a salesman. People have to like you and what you are selling. Use that same skill and translate it in new business ventures. One of the worst possible things that can happen to your music career is you becoming famous, but then you go broke and have to work a regular job. There's nothing wrong with working a regular job and providing for your family, but the goal of this book is for you to become successful in the music business, so that working regular jobs no longer have to become an option. Study other successful musicians' careers and find out what other business ventures they got involved with, after their musical success. Study and do research on what has worked for others. If you follow a winning formula, you really can't lose. The music business is very cool and very rewarding. Music is definitely a great segue business and it will open the doors to meeting new people from all walks of life. Collect as many business cards and contacts from the people you meet during your journey. Keep open and positive relationships with people and be as friendly as possible. People that you may randomly meet in the music business may later become very helpful in ways you may not be able to imagine.

If you are able to follow the instructions that I noted in this book, then you will see progress and ultimately see success. I hope this book was helpful and I hope that you got something out of it. Continue to study other people who have already had success and do not get discouraged.

19 FINAL THOUGHTS

The Internet is making it a lot easier for DIY artists and record labels to succeed. You can't win a game if you don't play it. The hardest step for most is simply getting started. Do not allow lack of finances and lack of resources hinder your creativity. The most creative work comes from those who are lacking proper resources. Set goals and plan for the future and you will not lose. Every goal that I have set in the music business, I have accomplished and I even superseded my expectations. I am now setting new goals and I plan to accomplish them all. Write down your goals on paper so that you can transfer you mental thoughts to a psychical piece of paper. Keep setting goals, short-term and long-term. Have faith in yourself and your team and continue to work hard.

Don't get too caught up in the production value. Some people focus so much on what they are lacking, that they never take the first step of simply putting out their creative work. It's hard at first and you may have to build up a level of confidence if you don't already possess it. The worst thing you can do, is not put your work out there. People will come up with all types of excuses for why not to put their unpolished work out there. Don't be one of those people. The best work in my opinion is the raw unpolished material. If you don't have a camera man with a good camera, then use your iPhone or cell phone to record your video content. The different between those who are successful and those who are not, is that the successful ones took the first step and initiated. Don't make excuses for why you aren't proceeding with your dreams. As time goes by and the older you get, it becomes harder and harder to get started, due to growing responsibilities. Do your best, try to be original, don't be afraid to copy others who are successful, be yourself and have faith in the unknown.

Thank you for reading this book. You have already taken the first step. If you have any questions about anything that I've written in this book, feel free to contact me.

Thank you

Ousala Aleem

ABOUT THE AUTHOR

Ousala Aleem , also known as Prestley Snipes and FD, is a Platinum selling and Grammy Award Nominated songwriter, filmmaker, director, producer, entertainment manager, photographer and entrepreneur. As a filmmaker and director for over 15 years, Ousala has worked with some of music's top artists and has 4 RIAA certified gold and platinum plaques to his credit. Ousala is best known for his independent film Criminals Gone Wild and for introducing ILoveMakonnen to the music scene. Ousala has worked with many top producers and artists including Drake, Mike Will Made It, Zaytoven, Polow Da Don, Metro Boomin, Sonny Digital, ILoveMakonnen, 2 Chainz, Noah "40" Shebib, Cap1, DJ Spinz, Dun Deal, Soulja Boy, Shawty Lo, Gucci Mane, Waka Flocka Flame, TM88, Southside of 808 Mafia, Wayne Wonder, Rae Sremmurd, Trinidad James, Safaree Samuels, Wiz Khalifa, Snoop Dogg, Neo Da Matrix and many more. He earned his first platinum plaque, with Drake, while managing and developing ILoveMakonnen. In 2015, Ousala was nominated for a Grammy Award for his co-writing, production and publishing contribution on the "Tuesday" song. In 2016, Ousala was honored at the 29th Annual ASCAP Rhythm And Soul Music Awards for "Tuesday" which was among the top ASCAP songs on the 2015 year-end charts. In 2016, Dutch DJ Burak Yeter released a cover of Ousala's song "Tuesday". Since then, Burak's version of "Tuesday" has become one of the top selling International Dance songs of 2016-2017 and has gone Platinum in Austria, the Netherlands, Russia, Germany, Finland and Switzerland. Ousala is currently managing the careers of several artists, songwriters, producers and entertainers.

Made in the USA
Columbia, SC
23 November 2018